CRITICAL PERSPECTIVES ON PRIVACY RIGHTS AND PROTECTIONS IN THE 21ST CENTURY

ANALYZING THE ISSUES

CRITICAL PERSPECTIVES ON PRIVACY RIGHTS AND PROTECTIONS IN THE 21ST CENTURY

Edited by Rita Santos

Enslow Publishing

101 W. 23rd Street
Suite 240
New York, NY 10011
USA

enslow.com

Published in 2019 by Enslow Publishing, LLC
101 W. 23rd Street, Suite 240, New York, NY 10011

Library of Congress Cataloging-in-Publication Data

Names: Santos, Rita, editor.
Title: Critical perspectives on privacy rights and protections in the 21st
  century / edited by Rita Santos.
Description: New York : Enslow Publishing, 2019. | Series: Analyzing the
  issues | Includes bibliographical references and index. | Audience: Grade
  7-12.
Identifiers: LCCN 2018002542| ISBN 9780766098572 (library bound) | ISBN
9780766098589 (pbk.)
Subjects: LCSH: Privacy, Right of—United States—Juvenile literature. |
Information society—United States—Juvenile literature. | Information
  technology—Social aspects—United States—Juvenile literature.
Classification: LCC JC596.2.U5 C75 2019 | DDC 323.44/80973—dc23
LC record available at https://lccn.loc.gov/2018002542

Printed in the United States of America

To Our Readers: We have done our best to make sure all website addresses
in this book were active and appropriate when we went to press. However,
the author and the publisher have no control over and assume no
liability for the material available on those websites or on any websites
they may link to. Any comments or suggestions can be sent by email to
customerservice@enslow.com.

Excerpts and articles have been reproduced with the permission of the
copyright holders.

Photo Credits: Cover, Anadolu Agency/Getty Images; cover and interior
pages graphics Thaiview/Shutterstock.com (cover top, pp. 3, 6-7), gbreezy/
Shutterstock.com (magnifying glass), Ghornstern/Shutterstock.com
(interior pages).

CONTENTS

INTRODUCTION

From the time we are small we're taught that some things are private, meant for a chosen few, and some things are public. Whether something is private or not can change depending on the situation you're in. For example, you might feel comfortable telling your best friend that you're afraid of squirrels but you probably don't want everyone in your class knowing. As we put more and more information online, including everything from health records to our family photographs, questions about what should remain private and when become complicated.

In 2013, Edward Snowden sparked a global debate about privacy after he leaked information about the true scope of the mass surveillance performed by the National Security Agency (NSA). In the debate that followed, many argued that government surveillance through data collection of American citizens violates the Fourth Amendment of the Constitution. Others saw it as a necessary step in the fight against terror.

The Fourth Amendment protects us against unreasonable searches by law enforcement. This means the police need to follow certain rules when searching people's homes, cars, or other property. Many wonder if electronic data should be subject to the same rules. As technology advances so, too, must our laws surrounding privacy. Websites have the ability to track and monitor the actions of users, even after they have left the webpage. Social media sites like Facebook and Twitter regularly collect and sell data or information about their users to advertisers without users' knowledge. American intelligence agencies now believe that foreign nations used social media ads and posts to influence the outcome of the 2016 presidential election. What role does our government have in protecting citizens from this kind of influence? Could mass surveillance prevent such activities or would it promote totalitarianism?

A popular argument among those in favor of mass surveillance is that law-abiding citizens have nothing to fear. However, historically, this has not always been true. In the 1930s and 1940s, the Nazis used census records to locate and exterminate Jewish people. The existence of the census wasn't necessarily dangerous, but how the Nazis used the information was. Data that identifies and locates people can always be abused in the wrong hands. Privacy rights help us control who has access to information about us and how they can use it.

Currently in the United States, digital data is owned by the person—or the organization—who collects it. When we create social media accounts, the information we post is collected by the social media companies. While most companies post their privacy policies, which sometimes explain what and how data is used, they are not required by law to do so. While everyone should read privacy policies before making accounts, most people do not. Advocacy groups like the American Civil Liberties Union (ACLU) and the

Electronic Privacy Information Center (EPIC) want citizens to have more control over their data. In the European Union (EU), people own their own data so companies must be more transparent about how they are collecting and using it. Many American advocacy groups believe the US should adopt similar laws.

Technology can sometimes advance faster than our laws and ethical standards can keep up. Sometimes tech companies can unknowingly create privacy issues in an attempt to use data to solve a problem. While tech companies must be held accountable when they put people's privacy in danger, they should also have guidance when trying to balance progress with the need for privacy.

In this book you will hear what people from different critical perspectives have to say on the topic of privacy rights in the twenty-first century. It is a topic every citizen should put some thought into. As you read, think about what privacy means to you and what kind of information you share every day. The information collected in this book can help you navigate the internet while keeping your data safe.

CHAPTER 1

WHAT THE ACADEMICS SAY

Laws typically reflect the ethics or morals of our society. As technology opens up new questions surrounding privacy rights, academics have a duty to provide possible answers. Some academics study history to show how data and privacy have been misused in the past, with the hope of preventing the use of similar tactics in the future. Other researchers are focused on finding out how technology is changing how our society feels about privacy and the consequences of this change. Academics study the many ways that data can be used to oppress or otherwise injure people. But they also study the ways that data can be used for the greater good. Data can be used to give researchers better insight into human behavior, which can help solve many social problems. It is the role of academia to explain what the right to privacy means and how we can protect it.

"PRIVACY IN THE AGE OF SURVEILLANCE," BY DINAH POKEMPNER, FROM *FOREIGN POLICY IN FOCUS*, FEBRUARY 17, 2014

A STRONG GLOBAL RIGHT TO ELECTRONIC PRIVACY DEMANDS RECOGNITION, IN U.S. LAW AND INTERNATIONALLY

President Obama had a signature opportunity in his January speech to limit the damage Edward Snowden's revelations about National Security Agency (NSA) surveillance had done to U.S. foreign relations. But global response has been rather cool.

Obama called for increased transparency and an institutional advocate for civil liberties before the secret court that oversees the NSA. He recognized that foreigners have an interest in the privacy of their communications. And he announced future restrictions on the use of acquired data as well as his hope to move data storage out of the NSA's hands. Yet he made clear he did not intend to end bulk collection of data or give foreigners legal rights to defend their privacy against unwarranted U.S. spying.

A month later, European and Brazilian efforts to turn the screws on U.S. companies over data protection continue full steam, and foreign officials remain skeptical of U.S. intentions. Snowden received eight Nobel Prize nominations from around the world. On the domestic front, many also found Obama's speech wanting ("It was a nothing burger" was legal scholar Jonathan Turley's memorable take).

In a world where almost all aspects of daily social and economic life have migrated online, the right to privacy has gained in importance, and not just for the paranoid few. It is a necessity for human rights activists and ordinary citizens around the world to freely speak, think, and associate without restrictions imposed by those who might wish to silence or harm them. At the same time, corporations and governments have acquired frightening abilities to amass and search these endless digital records.

The United States, once at the forefront of promoting the right to privacy as essential to modern life, has lagged behind in legal protection even as its spying prowess has burgeoned. As a model, this is ominous, for other nations are working hard to emulate U.S. surveillance capability by bringing more and more data within their reach.

There will be no safe haven if privacy is seen as a strictly domestic issue, and legal doctrine stays stuck in pre-digital time. A strong global right to electronic privacy demands recognition, in U.S. law and internationally.

A SHORT HISTORY OF PRIVACY

The United States early developed a private legal "right to be let alone." Suits against unwanted intrusion or exploitation of private details were popular, but the press fought back and often won on free expression grounds. Europe's law often put more emphasis on reputational rights.

World War II and the rise of modern surveillance states gave impetus to privacy as a defense against government abuse. The Third Reich mined census data to carry forward its genocidal policies. Many authoritarian states also deployed elaborate surveillance and data collection systems to cow their populations and suppress dissent — practices still used in places like China, Vietnam, Iran, and Ethiopia.

Privacy was invoked to limit the government's power of search and seizure. Judicially authorized warrants became a common requirement in many legal systems, and the notion of privacy of "correspondence" broadened to include new technologies, such as telephones, with laws regulating wiretaps.

THE TECHNOLOGICAL CHALLENGE

Yet protections often lagged behind technological change. In the 1928 *Olmstead* case, the Supreme Court held that an unauthorized wiretap did not violate the constitutional right of the people "to be secure in their persons, houses, papers, and effects." In 1967, the court reversed course, determining that a person has "reasonable expectation of privacy" when talking in a public phone booth. This bit of common sense developed into a doctrine for when to limit government power to conduct warrantless searches.

The doctrine, however, has not always produced decisions that reflect common sense or popular expectations. Courts tend to focus more on what they think is reasonable for public safety. You may not expect warrantless aerial surveillance of your backyard, but the Supreme Court thinks that's fine, provided that what the camera sees can be observed by the naked eye. Similarly, courts have ruled that we have no expectation of privacy for information we share as business records — phone or credit card transactions, for example. Never mind that refusing to convey such information essentially bars us from engaging in many realms of modern life.

When the administration disavows indiscriminately reviewing your "private" information, it means it considers the "metadata" — the where-when-who-how long and even subject of your communications — to be "business records," no matter how detailed a portrait this provides of your daily life.

U.S. law has grown to equate privacy of communications with secrecy, an approach "ill-suited to the digital age," Justice Sonia Sotomayor said recently in a case that rejected police GPS monitoring of a vehicle for weeks on end without a warrant.

Louis Brandeis, who as a young lawyer practically invented U.S. privacy law, warned of the lag between technological leaps and doctrine. Dissenting in *Olmstead*, he wrote: "Ways may someday be developed by which the Government, without removing papers from secret drawers, can reproduce them in court, and by which it will be enabled to expose to a jury the most intimate occurrences of the home." Maybe in 1928 this sounded futuristic, but post-Snowden it seems weirdly prescient. Wiretaps eventually required warrants, but electronic surveillance metastasized in the 21st century under a secret regime of indulgent, minimalist judicial supervision.

A DIFFERENT PATH

The law in Europe took a different path. In 1983, the German Constitutional Court annulled the national census law, announcing "informational self-determina-

tion" as a fundamental democratic right. Integral to the
modern European approach has been the belief that
individuals have a right to access and correct their data
held by various institutions, and ultimately to determine
its use and disposal.

This approach to informational self-
determination has found some parallel in a different
branch of privacy jurisprudence. Key decisions around
the world striking down sodomy laws and other aspects
of physical autonomy have also invoked privacy, not
simply as a "right to be left alone" but as a right to
establish one's identity and chosen relations. This rela-
tional view of privacy is essential to protecting minorities, dissidents, and freethinkers from persecution, not
to mention simply enabling the rest of us to work out
who we are and what we think.

Another area where the United States led was
connecting anonymity — the ultimate data protection —
to freedom of speech. No doubt it helped that many of
the nation's founders published revolutionary manifestos
under pseudonyms. In April, the UN special rapporteur
on the promotion and protection of the right to freedom
of opinion, Frank LaRue, decried the "chilling effect" that
restrictions on anonymity have had on the free expression
of information and ideas

The value of anonymous speech has only become
more apparent in the wake of the shift of many aspects of
modern life online, and the breakthroughs in our ability to
store, search, collate, and analyze data with minimal cost.
Anonymity now seems a last defense for both privacy and
the many rights to which digital privacy provides access
— such as speech, association, belief, and health.

CLOSING THE LOOPHOLES

Snowden's revelations of massive global surveillance inflamed an existing debate about what constitutes mass surveillance and whether it is ever justified. To understand how we got there, the loopholes knit into U.S. law are as critical to understand as the technological backdoors.

The first loophole is that the United States does not consider itself bound, when its actions pose harm abroad, to respect foreigners' rights in the way the Constitution requires it to respect rights at home. Moreover, the United States tries to limit its obligations under international human rights law in the same way. Although the president may choose to selectively limit data collection for reasons of comity (calling rather than bugging Angela Merkel, for example), ordinary foreigners who pose no conceivable threat to U.S. interests can't legally challenge U.S. dragnet surveillance of their communications. Of course, the data of many U.S. citizens gets swept up in the dragnet too.

Another big loophole is that the United States considers digital metadata to be only business records, subject to little protection. Under section 215 of the Patriot Act, these records can be collected if they are merely "relevant" to investigating terrorism, counterespionage, or foreign intelligence generally—and we already know the surveillance court thought virtually all U.S. call records fit that standard.

The administration has also staked a position that use, not acquisition, is the point where data privacy is at stake. But the legal view in Europe is different, and few take comfort in the notion of a foreign entity collecting their data without permission so long as no one has read it (yet).

Several domestic lawsuits — including one to which Human Rights Watch is a party — are challenging this point.

Unfortunately, nothing President Obama said would really close these loopholes tightly. And nothing has yet begun to address the breach of trust caused by recent allegations that the United States systematically tried to weaken strong encryption standards, use back-door access to technology and cable flows, or in other ways subvert the very architecture of privacy on the Internet.

GLOBAL RESPONSE

Stung by U.S. monitoring of their leaders, Germany and Brazil co-sponsored a successful UN General Assembly resolution that asked the UN human rights expert to report on the harm caused by mass surveillance to privacy.

These issues will soon come before the UN Human Rights Council, the General Assembly, the European Court of Human Rights, and the U.S. Supreme Court. It would be wise for the Obama administration to modify its positions before these considerations reach the point of condemnation.

The administration can do so by immediately ending its indiscriminate, bulk interception programs, giving foreigners the same protections as citizens against unjustified invasion of privacy, ending efforts to weaken privacy protections in both the technical and legal domain, and proposing laws to help these changes survive into the next administration.

And it might help if Obama found a way to enable the man who started the debate — Edward Snowden — to come home without fearing a lifetime in prison. After all, one day they may both be Nobel laureates.

1. How might anonymity, or the ability to keep one's identity private, encourage freedom of speech?

2. Should the constitutional right to privacy extend to foreign citizens?

EXCERPT FROM "THE RIGHT TO PRIVACY," FROM BOUNDLESS POLITICAL SCIENCE AT LUMEN LEARNING

BACKGROUND

United States privacy law embodies several different legal concepts. One is the invasion of privacy. It is a tort based in common law allowing an aggrieved party to bring a lawsuit against an individual who unlawfully intrudes into his or her private affairs, discloses his or her private information, publicizes him or her in a false light, or appropriates his or her name for personal gain.

The Right to Privacy is a law review article written by Samuel Warren and Louis Brandeis. It was published in the 1890 *Harvard Law Review*. It is one of the most influential essays in the history of American law. The article is widely regarded as the first publication in the United States to advocate a right to privacy, articulating that right primarily as a right to be left alone. It was written primarily by Louis Brandeis although credited to both men, on a suggestion of Warren based on his deep-seated abhorrence of the invasions of social privacy. William Prosser, in writing his own influential article on the privacy torts in American law, attributed the specific incident to an intrusion by journalists on a society wedding. However, in truth it was inspired by more general coverage of intimate personal lives in society columns of newspapers.

DEFINING THE NECESSITY OF THE RIGHT TO PRIVACY

The authors begin the article by noting that it has been found necessary from time to time to define anew the exact nature and extent of the individual's protections of person and property. The article states that the scope of such legal rights broadens over time -- to now include the right to enjoy life -- the right to be left alone.

Then the authors point out the conflicts between technology and private life. They note that recent inventions and business methods, such as instant pictures and newspaper enterprise have invaded domestic life, and numerous mechanical devices may make it difficult to enjoy private communications.

The authors discuss a number of cases involving photography, before turning to the law of trade secrets. Finally, they conclude that the law of privacy extends beyond contractual principles or property rights. Instead, they state that it is a right against the world.

REMEDIES AND DEFENSES

The authors consider the possible remedies available. They also mention the necessary limitations on the doctrine, excluding matters of public or general interest, privileged communications such as judicial testimony, oral publications in the absence of special damage, and publications of information published or consented to by the individual. They pause to note that defenses within the law of defamation -- the truthfulness of the information published or the absence of the publisher's malice -- should not be defenses. Finally, they propose as remedies the availability of tort actions for damages and possible injunctive relief.

MODERN TORT LAW

In the United States today, "invasion of privacy" is a commonly used cause of action in legal pleadings. Modern tort law includes four categories of invasion of privacy:

- Intrusion of solitude: physical or electronic intrusion into one's private quarters
- Public disclosure of private facts: the dissemination of truthful private information which a reasonable person would find objectionable
- False light: the publication of facts which place a person in a false light, even though the facts themselves may not be defamatory
- Appropriation: the unauthorized use of a person's name or likeness to obtain some benefits.

CONSTITUTIONAL BASIS FOR RIGHT TO PRIVACY

The Constitution only protects against state actors. Invasions of privacy by individuals can only be remedied under previous court decisions.

The Fourth Amendment to the Constitution of the United States ensures the right of the people to be secure in their persons, houses, papers and effects, against unreasonable searches and seizures, shall not be violated, and no warrants shall issue, but upon probable cause, supported by oath or affirmation, and particularly describing the place to be searched, and the persons or things to be seized.

The First Amendment protects the right to free assembly, broadening privacy rights. The Ninth Amendment declares the fact that if a right is not explicitly mentioned in the Constitution it does not mean that the government can infringe on that right. The Supreme Court recognized the 14th Amendment as providing a substantive due process right to privacy. This was first recognized by several Supreme Court Justices in *Griswold v. Connecticut*, a 1965 decision protecting a married couple's rights to contraception. It was recognized again in 1973 *Roe v. Wade*, which invoked the right to privacy in order to protect a woman's right to an abortion.

1. Why is the right to privacy also known as "the right to be left alone"?

2. What does invasion of privacy mean?

"THE IMPORTANCE OF INFORMED CONSENT IN SOCIAL MEDIA RESEARCH," BY DR. ILKA GLEIBS, FROM THE LONDON SCHOOL OF ECONOMICS AND POLITICAL SCIENCE IMPACT BLOG, MARCH 27, 2015

Informed consent is important in large-scale social media research to protect the privacy, autonomy, and control of social media users. Ilka Gleibs argues for an approach to consent that fosters contextual integrity where adequate protection for privacy is tied to specific contexts. Rather than prescribing universal rules for what is public (a Facebook page, or Twitter feed) and what is private, contextual integrity builds from within the normative bounds of a given context and illustrates why researchers must attend to the context in information flows and its use when thinking about research ethics.

During the US mid-term elections in 2010, the news feeds of all US Facebook users changed subtly: Without users' knowledge, researchers manipulated the feeds' to show whom of their friends had already voted – for some users this included a picture of those friends, for some it didn't. Subsequently, this information was matched with the voter-records to understand who actually went out to vote and whether this was depending on their friends' behavior. This 61-million-person experiment investigating social influence and voting behavior and was published by Adam Kramer, a Facebook data scientist, and colleagues in *Nature* last year.

This year Adam Kramer and his colleagues published another large-scale experiment that manipulated the feeds' emotional content and examined how Facebook friends' emotions affected one another. The later study on "massive-scale emotional contagion through social networks" generated significant debate in both public and scientific spheres. Even the editor-in-chief of *PNAS*, where the study was published, voiced concern that the "collection of the data by Facebook may have involved practices that were not fully consistent with the principles of obtaining fully informed consent and allowing participants to opt out".

Whether these studies were in essence unethical is a matter of debate. Both studies (and others that use large-scale social media data) largely followed ethical guidelines of their institutions (Facebook, Cornell University, and UC San Diego). In addition, Facebook's terms of agreement make it clear that research may be conducted and (legally) users who sign off the terms of agreement give consent. Lastly, one could argue that that an online environment (for example messages on the home page like the newsfeed in Facebook) is constantly altered and changed for marketing and web-development reasons. Thus, the researchers argued that anticipated harm of no direct informed consent (the explicit permission of taking part in a study) did not outweigh the benefits of scientific discovery.

Yet, most of the critics pointed out that it was problematic that Facebook users were part of a study without their knowledge. Many Facebook 'users' (or 'potential participants) felt concerned or even betrayed after publication of results. Thus, it seems that many people would have liked to be informed that they were part of an experiment and would have appreciated a more comprehensive form of consent. This highlights that the subjective expectations of consent might not always match the legal and institutional requirements that organizations follow and raises questions on how we conduct studies with large-scale data from social media platforms and hence their research ethics.

In a recently published paper in *Analysis of Social Issues and Public Policy* I focus on this question of the appropriate role of informed consent in large-scale online studies. Informed consent is an important cornerstone of ethical research that has important implication of using data from social media platforms and I argued that informed consent is (still) vital for conducting large-scale experiments to protect the privacy, autonomy, and control of users and ultimately our participants.

Based on the concept of privacy in context (Nissenbaum, 2009), I propose that this is because the norms of distribution and appropriateness are violated when researchers manipulate online contexts and collect data without consent. Contextual integrity refers to a theory of privacy in which the protection of personal information is linked to the norms of information flow in a specific context. Thus, contextual integrity ties adequate protection for privacy to norms in a specific context. In essence, it demands that information collection and its dissemination should be appropriate to the context (Nissenbaum, 2004). For example, in a healthcare context, patients expect to share personal information on their health and they most likely accept that this information is shared with a specialist. Their expectations are violated, however, if they learn that the information is sold to a marketing company.

Rather than prescribing universal rules for what is public (a Facebook page, or Twitter feed) and what is private, contextual integrity builds from within the normative bounds of a given context and illustrates why we must attend to the context in information flows and its use— not the nature of the information itself—when thinking about research ethics. Thus, it is this difference in how the information flow is perceived by researchers (as accessible and easy to 'manipulate') and by users (as private and shared only among 'friends') that creates the ethical tension and which should be taken into account when we make ethical decisions on the use of SNS data.

To go back to the studies that stirred the controversy; whereas users or participants expected to share information with their known social circle (i.e., similar to telling a friend how I feel today, or whether I voted), the flow of information was changed in the way that this information was modified and responses were studied and then widely published (without consent). Thus, in the "faceless" context of online experiment, the users became "human subjects" and Facebook an experimental field; turning a virtual space into a virtual laboratory. Thus, changing and using information on the newsfeed or personal profiles for research purpose that is geared toward behavioral change impacted on the autonomy and freedom of participants. This is troublesome (and many users picked up on this) because it harms the perception of control and autonomy (which could be witnessed in the many negative responses especially to the second paper). Moreover, it threatens the trust between the community of social scientists and participants, which might have been another reason for the many concerned voices after the publication of the articles. From this standpoint the control of information and what is done with it seems crucial for the management of privacy and autonomy concerns and the ethical handling of research in SNS and has to be discussed in light of the overall values of the context.

Thus, I think that informed consent is vital for conducting large-scale experiments to protect the privacy, autonomy, and control of users and ultimately our participants. Lack of ethical research can hinder academic progress, our regard as a community and trustworthiness. We ultimately need an earnest, innovative and creative discussion in the field on how to implement ethical guidelines that first and foremost protect participants but also allow researchers to conduct sound research. I propose that we start to reconsider the conceptions of risk, benefit and harm of potential participants (e.g. SNS users) and treat participants as stakeholder in research and not passive objects we observe. Various potential ways of gaining consent are discussed my article.

Researchers, ethics committees, and funders must reconsider current approaches to consent to live up to the challenges provided by large-scale online experiments. Shapiro and Ossorio warned that the private sector is charging ahead and de facto creates standards for data use that provide broad — I would argue overly broad — access to personal information and behavior. As a field we should make sure that our work has social value that goes beyond selling products and that we are on the front line of setting standards for accessing and working with people's online information that are in line with our ethical consciousness and research practice.

1. Do you think it's ethical for social media sites like Facebook to conduct experiments on users without informing them?

2. What is contextual integrity? Why is it important?

"DATA AND PROTECTING THE RIGHT TO PRIVACY," BY JENNIFER GRANICK, FROM THE CENTER FOR INTERNET AND SOCIETY, SEPTEMBER 29, 2015

Privacy's obituary has been written many, many times, but the patient lingers on. One of the most famous law review articles of all time, "The Right to Privacy," was written in 1890 about a new camera that could make images without the subject holding a still pose. The authors, Samuel Warren and Louis Brandeis, lamented this invasive development and recommended that privacy invasions be classified as a tort—a social wrong for which there would be an economic remedy.

Today we hear the similar lament: Privacy is dead. But unlike Brandeis and Warren, we aren't pushing hard for legal protections for our personal information. Instead, we're giving up. Elderly Luddites wag a finger at young people for using Facebook and other social apps. We are told to "get over it" if we want cool new innovations.

Privacy does not have to be an all or nothing thing. Sure, technology is changing privacy, but law can help.

We can legislate greater protections to counterbalance the privacy harms of new technologies, while still enjoying their benefits. And we'd better act quickly, because a range of new cool devices is about to come online and blow privacy out of the water.

Everything you do online is trackable, from the websites you read, to your search queries, to your social networking posts. Enjoying the fruits of modern living means unintentionally and unavoidably spilling tons of sensitive information. It's not just using Facebook or online gaming. Search queries, Web browsing, online banking reveal our interests, our reading, our finances, and more.

The data shedding is only going to get worse. Increasingly, our offline activities will create a data trail, too. Cellphones track our physical location through space and time. More and more of the everyday appliances we use are networked together and connected to the Internet. The business buzzword for this is the "Internet of Things." The term means that hardware devices such as your stove, your thermostat, your car, which were originally stand-alone machines will be controlled through the Internet. These innovations are awesome. I can preheat the oven before I get home from work. I can get an estimate to fix my car without having to go into the shop. But these connected devices take our offline physical lives and make them digital and networked. In short, they become subject to surveillance. The heat was off all weekend, so we are probably out of town. I stopped going to church, perhaps I am having a crisis of faith. My Fitbit says I'm not sleeping. Is my insomnia indicative of a health problem? Burglars, gossips and insurance companies all may want to use these things against us in improper ways.

What's worse is that while the corporate collection of data allows for free online services and new discoveries, it is a funnel for information to flow to the U.S. and other governments, entities that do not always act responsibly or respectfully of human rights. Certainly, surveillance data is used to go after criminals, drug dealers and tax cheats. But U.S. police officers and intelligence agents also use such data to monitor Muslim Americans and social movements such as Occupy Wall Street and Black Lives Matter. If this happens in the U.S. just think about how bad it's going to be for the next billion Internet users, who will almost all come from countries that do not have a Bill of Rights or a First Amendment.

We must not just throw our hands in the air and give up. That's what the data brokers demanding endless permissions to collect and crunch information about us for targeted advertising and for resale to insurance and financial companies want. That's what law enforcement and intelligence agencies eager to "Collect It All" want, frictionless spying. But that's not what's good for a democracy or for human rights.

Targeted surveillance focusing on suspected criminals and terrorists is necessary and appropriate, but right now surveillance is sweeping—without judicial supervision, probable cause or individualized suspicion. There are legal bills right now languishing in Congress that would protect email and your physical location from warrantless searches. This legislation should be passed. Further, we need to expand privacy protections to cover buddy lists, drive backups, social networking posts, Web browsing history, medical data, bank records, face prints, voice prints, driving patterns, DNA and more.

Good laws can ensure that the U.S. government only gets information when there's good cause, and not for trolling or social oppression.

Of course, U.S. privacy law isn't going to help vulnerable people in other countries—homosexuals in India, religious minorities in Saudi Arabia or human rights workers in Syria. These people need to be able to trust their secrets to the technology they use. But the U.S. fights against secure cellphones and online services in favor of insecure, surveillance-friendly networks that oppressive governments can access and which put people around the world at risk. The U.S. plan is to risk individual safety in exchange for maintaining and growing its surveillance advantages. That's wrong, and shortsighted.

Privacy is at a crossroads, and we have to make important decisions. Are we going to give up, or are we going to use the tools at our disposal to protect privacy and security? We have to stop overriding the few privacy laws we have to gain a false sense of online security. We have to utterly reject secret surveillance laws, if only because secret law is an abomination in a democracy. We have to secure, not undermine, communications networks for people around the globe. Are we going to do any of these things?

1. What are some of the dangers posed to privacy by the "Internet of Things"?

2. How do surveillance-friendly technological networks pose risks to those living under oppressive governments?

"IS DIGITAL CONNECTIVITY THREATENING YOUR PRIVACY?," BY JENNIFER THOMAS, FROM THE UNIVERSITY OF MELBOURNE: *PURSUIT*, MARCH 14, 2017

THE INTERNET OF THINGS (IOT) IS CONNECTING US LIKE NEVER BEFORE, BUT AT WHAT COST?

It is 11:15 am and you are in the middle of a doctor's appointment when a reminder message for your Melbourne to Sydney flight that departs in two hours, pops up on your mobile phone. It warns you that with the current traffic conditions you will need to leave your location in the next 10 minutes to ensure you don't miss your flight. It is the first time you have received a message like this and for a moment you wonder where this message comes from. Is this a time saving service, or an invasion of privacy?

A team of researchers from the Melbourne Networked Society Institute, led by Dr Rachelle Bosua and Professor Megan Richardson, have conducted a qualitative research project to discover how IoT users and developers view 'privacy' and the adequacy of current legal regulations to protect individuals' privacy.

The study has found that both IoT technology users and developers lack understanding about the privacy issues involved with personal data collection and storage. In their haste to access new services, users often do not read the fine print and consent forms are often overly lengthy and jargon-filled. Equally many technology developers seem unaware of their legal obligations when it comes to safely seeking, using and storing people's data.

Dr. Bosua, from the School of Computing and Information Systems, and Professor Richardson, from the Melbourne Law School, suggest some modest changes could go a long way to securing our data, without threatening the benefits we receive from technological innovation.

Simple measures can ensure developers collect minimal data, are transparent about how data is used and stored, and use consent forms that are easy to understand, reducing the risk of hacking and other breaches of privacy. They also recommend that embedding legal aspects into the design and development of software should be taught as part of the curriculum.

The mobile devices we carry track most of our movements and gather data about our location that we aren't aware of, possibly through apps that we haven't added or don't even actively use. More often than not, we receive IoT services, without being asked if we would like them.

To gain access to IoT enabled services, there is a vast amount of data being collected, some of which can be personal. Many of us are willing to give away our personal data in return for a service, but are we always aware of what we are giving away, how it will be used, and if it will be stored securely once collected?

Dr. Bosua and her team conducted interviews with IoT technology users and developers to discover how they felt about the potential privacy issues surrounding their use of these technologies.

"Initially IoT users spoke in favor of the IoT devices they were using, focusing on the benefits, such as convenience and connectivity that they provided; most seemed unaware or unconcerned about privacy issues," she says.

It was only as the interviews progressed that Dr. Bosua noted users started to voice some concern about their privacy, as they became more aware of potential problems.

"By the end of the interview many users admitted they were no longer sure about their views on privacy, most felt that they did want more control, and better understanding of how their data was being used and why."

Many reported that they wanted consent forms to be shorter and simpler and written in plain English.

"Users want to know how and why their data is being used, along with some guarantee that private data will be stored securely and not be vulnerable to hacking."

Interviews with IoT developers and designers found they were also deficient in their knowledge of the privacy issues involved with data collection, usage and storage.

"We discovered there could be many young entrepreneurs, who aren't fully aware of the right thing to do from a legal perspective. Compliance doesn't seem to be an issue at the moment either," explains Dr. Bosua.

She is keen to see some reform to the regulations protecting privacy in regards to the IoT, but does not want to stifle technological innovation, acknowledging IoT developers are creating innovative solutions and services that can be of huge benefit to our lives. She believes privacy can be protected by some simple changes, such as moving towards a model of privacy by design, in which a minimum standard of data protection is guaranteed, and enforcing more transparent standards.

Teaching IoT developers to apply privacy by design should be the default position, she says.

"We must start with educating developers about privacy and this should begin with the education system."

But why is privacy online so important? When you sign up for a new IoT service and provide your data, it flows into the digital domain, and forms a digital footprint of who you are. Your digital footprint has a long lifespan and can give a misleading impression of who you are today. Youthful mistakes may live on in the cyber world, long after they have ceased to have any meaning or relevance to you, and can cause damage.

"Potential employers often check social websites before hiring staff, which can lead to people having real regrets if they have given too much of their privacy away," Dr. Bosua says.

The tools that analyze big data are getting smarter and can recognize patterns in data to make inferences about users. So, for example, if you are a person that regularly sees the doctor, a negative inference could be made about your state of health, which could increase your health insurance premium.

In a world that is so reliant on online service delivery, hacking has become a major problem. Cybersecurity will become more and more crucial as time goes on.

"More robust security tools focusing on small devices will need to be developed and I think as our awareness of buying things and getting access to services increases, we will become more careful about security and privacy," says Dr. Bosua.

Dr. Bosua suggests the development of a locking system could be beneficial, so that very personal data could be locked down more securely and data that is not as important, could have less strict controls applied. For example, extremely private data such as health data that may be used by a personal medical device such as a wirelessly enabled pacemaker or a drug infusion pump, would require a very secure lock, whereas wellness data collected through a device such as a Fitbit, might not need such secure locking.

While hacked wellness data may result in a higher health insurance premium, hacking into a medical device could actually lead to someone's death and was the reason former US Vice President Dick Cheney had the wireless capability of his pacemaker disabled.

Dr. Bosua says the only reason that stricter regulation and more transparency has not been required in Australia to date, is that nothing has gone badly wrong yet.

"We have gone a bit out of control with the information that is online, but often the law kicks in when things go wrong. People don't have a good awareness of what they are giving away and asking the right questions such as: do I need this service? Is it legal? Will they use my data with protection and security in mind, or not? We need to be more aware and start doing this differently."

1. Why does the author argue that transparency is needed in regard to the use and collection of data?

2. Why would a data locking system be beneficial?

"THE DYNAMIC BALANCE BETWEEN FREE SPEECH AND PRIVACY INTERESTS," BY SARAH HINCHLIFF PEARSON, FROM THE CENTER FOR INTERNET AND SOCIETY AT STANFORD UNIVERSITY, APRIL 17, 2009

There have been a host of apocalyptic warnings in the blogosphere about the First Circuit's recent decision holding that truth is not an absolute defense to a defamation claim. One blogger dubbed it "the most dangerous libel decision in decades," and nearly everyone predicts it could have serious implications for journalists. But instead of joining the chorus of First Amendment advocates decrying the decision, I propose we take a step back to calmly examine the appropriate level of First Amendment protection for truthful private information.

The argument that individuals should be able to legally prevent third parties from revealing true information about them has an eerie similarity to trademark protection. Do we want to live in a culture where people have the legal right to police their reputations from inconvenient truths – a society full of tightly controlled human brands? The concept of being defamed by the truth seems in many ways to be the outgrowth of hyper-commercialization, reflecting a warped value system where image is valued more highly than honesty.

Yet, in an age where one-to-many communication is available to anyone with an Internet connection, it is reasonable to rethink the protection we grant to private, truthful information. The idea that private information is legally protectable is nothing new – we have privacy torts to protect embarrassing facts from disclosure under limited circumstances. But reasonable privacy interests aren't limited to objectively embarrassing facts. To maintain meaningful interpersonal relationships, we rely on our ability to control how and when we communicate our thoughts and personal information to different audiences, and in this sense, privacy is essential to human bonding. To the extent that technology threatens our ability to maintain compartmentalized lives, there are legitimate reasons to at least remain open to rethinking the way we balance First Amendment and privacy interests.

It is undeniable that privacy interests weigh more heavily against First Amendment rights when the information in question is not of public concern. The question then hinges on the potential chilling effect on free speech due to the uncertainty of whether a court would deem particular information newsworthy. But that chilling effect must be weighed against the risk that our private information will be disclosed to the public, a risk that is dramatically increased by the Internet. In other words, in a world where everyone is a publisher, traditional media outlets are no longer the primary concern of defamation law. It is one thing to rely on professional editors to exercise editorial judgment and quite another to rely on your neighbor.

That being said, privacy concerns relating to individual communicative preferences seem best regulated by social norms rather than the legal system. No one wants to live in a society that gives someone a legal remedy every time they object to their friend posting a kernel of truthful information about them on Facebook. But it would be unreasonable not to admit that our zones of personal privacy, the extent of control we have to tailor what we reveal to different audiences and through what relationships, are and will continue to be altered by technology. Whether this forces us to strike a new balance between freedom of speech and privacy interests remains to be seen, but we should recognize that this balance is not predetermined.

1. How does freedom of speech sometimes conflict with the right to privacy?

2. Should online privacy rights be regulated through social norms or the legal system?

"#NOTJUSTDORMS. THE FOURTH AMENDMENT: SECURITY, PRIVACY AND TECHNOLOGY," BY CONNIE FRAZIER AND DAVID NGUYEN, FROM *HIGHEREDUCATIONLAW*, JUNE 17, 2017

"The right of the people to be secure in their persons, houses, papers and effects against unreasonable searches and seizures, shall not be violated and no warrant shall issue, but upon probable cause, supported by an Oath or affirmation, and particularly describing the place to be searched, and the persons or things to be seized."

For over 200 years, the words of the Fourth Amendment have protected individual rights to privacy and provided safeguards against unreasonable governmental search and seizure. On college campuses, Fourth Amendment discussions are largely centered on residence halls or student conduct processes. However, advances in technology and the prevalence of electronic surveillance and monitoring present new challenges for colleges and the courts as they attempt to balance the need to provide enhanced security against individual rights to privacy. Has interpretation of the Fourth Amendment kept pace with technology and life in a surveillance state?

Katz v. United States (1967) was a landmark decision that clarified several key points; it concluded that the Fourth Amendment "protects people not places," that what a person "seeks to preserve as private, even an area accessible to the public, may be constitutionally protected" and finally, that unlawful surveillance need not physically penetrate a space. Foreshadowing FISA, Justices Douglas and Brennen, in concurring, further expressed concern that the ruling not be construed to offer a "green light for the Executive Branch to resort to electronic eaves-dropping without a warrant in cases which the Executive Branch itself labels 'national security' matters."

Keeping *Katz* in mind, fast forward to the vast array of electronic monitoring, surveillance and modern technology available in everyday life. These technological advances may force a reinterpretation of Fourth Amendment protections and legal process, particularly as it pertains to "plain view" and limited scope of search. Digital media after all, may be stored in the ambiguous and amorphous "cloud" and its actual content may not be readily apparent by simply looking at a document or file name. A 2013 article in the *Suffolk University Law Review* provides an interesting overview of the challenges of "plain view" and digital evidence and discusses the impact of Rule 41 of the Federal Rules of Criminal Procedure. Rule 41 has become a flashpoint in the debate over law enforcement assertions that such intrusions are necessary in order to maintain security versus those who argue that they represent too great a threat to individual civil liberties.

A specific example where law and regulation may be in conflict with the intended protections of the Fourth Amendment is the Stored Communications Act (SCA). While intended to bolster Fourth Amendment rights within the context of digital media, the language of the SCA was written before the creation of smart phones, social media and cloud computing its language does not take into account how these changes have changed the nature of digital content and privacy. Attempts to amend and update the SCA have failed in recent years. The SCA has also been a factor in cases where search of cell phone data incident to an arrest has been at issue. Under established interpretation, potentially incriminating evidence or items found on the individual's person may be allowed under "reasonable search." But what about the contents on a cell phone found incident to an arrest? Confusion and contradictory rulings on this subject in *People v. Diaz, State v. Smith* and others, ultimately led the U.S. Supreme Court to weigh in on the matter. In *Riley v California*, Chief Justice Roberts delivered the opinion, which perhaps hints at the Court's leanings regarding future privacy and search and seizure cases related to digital communication:

> *Modern cell phones are not just another technological convenience. With all they contain and all they may reveal, they hold for many Americans "the privacies of life," Boyd, supra,*

at 630, 6 S.Ct. 524. The fact that technology now allows an individual to carry such information in his hand does not make the information any less worthy of the protection for which the Founders fought. Our answer to the question of what police must do before searching a cell phone seized incident to an arrest is accordingly simple — get a warrant.

Tensions between privacy and security also play out on campuses. Recent high-profile incidents of student protest have exerted pressure on campuses to be more "transparent" and to show that they are "doing something" to address real and perceived threats. In response, there has been a proliferation of electronic surveillance and monitoring on campuses. Debate involving the use of CCTVs, electronic access, monitoring social media accounts, police body cameras and electronic or network use policies are entering into campus administrative policy debates. As the balance between security and privacy becomes more tenuous, it behooves administrators to be mindful of legal challenges to traditional interpretations of the Fourth Amendment and the implication they may have for policy and campus governance beyond residence halls and student conduct.

1. Is electronic surveillance and monitoring on school campuses a violation of students' right to privacy?

2. Why is the Stored Communications Act outdated?

CHAPTER 2

WHAT THE GOVERNMENT AND POLITICIANS SAY

American intelligence agencies believe that foreign governments used social media to influence the outcome of the 2016 presidential election. Facebook's use of personal data allowed foreign agents to send propaganda directly to people who were most likely to believe it. The government has a duty to protect citizens from physical threats, but what about cyber threats? Does the government have the same responsibility to protect citizens' digital privacy? At the same time, the American government was also quasi-legally using the National Security Agency (NSA) for mass surveillance. This leads many to wonder what the government's role is when it comes to digital privacy. Governments are asking themselves if it is possible to protect the privacy of citizens while also using tools of mass surveillance, and politicians are currently attempting to make laws to better define and protect privacy rights. The following articles will show how governments from around the world are dealing with issues of privacy in the twenty-first century.

"NEW UN RESOLUTION ON THE RIGHT TO PRIVACY IN THE DIGITAL AGE: CRUCIAL AND TIMELY," BY DEBORAH BROWN, FROM THE *INTERNET POLICY REVIEW*, NOVEMBER 22, 2016

The rapid pace of technological development enables individuals all over the world to use new information and communications technologies (ICTs) to improve their lives. At the same time, technology is enhancing the capacity of governments, companies and individuals to undertake surveillance, interception and data collection, which may violate or abuse human rights, in particular the right to privacy. In this context, the UN General Assembly's Third Committee adoption on 21 November of a new resolution on the right to privacy in the digital age comes as timely and crucial for protecting the right to privacy in light of new challenges.

As with previous UN resolutions on this topic, the resolution adopted on 21 November 2016 recognizes the importance of respecting international commitments in relation to the right to privacy. It underscores that any legitimate concerns states may have with regard to their security can and should be addressed in a manner consistent with obligations under international human rights law.

Recognizing that more and more personal data is being collected, processed, and shared, this year's resolution expresses concern about the sale or multiple re-sales of personal data, which often happens without the individual's free, explicit and informed consent. It calls for the strengthening of prevention of and protection against such violations, and calls on states to develop preventative measures, sanctions, and remedies.

This year, the resolution more explicitly acknowledges the role of the private sector. It calls on states to put in place (or maintain) effective sanctions and remedies to prevent the private sector from committing violations and abuses of the right to privacy. This is in line with states' obligations under the UN Guiding Principles on Business and Human Rights, which require states to protect against abuses by businesses within their territories or jurisdictions. The resolution specifically calls on states to refrain from requiring companies to take steps that interfere with the right to privacy in an arbitrary or unlawful way. With respect to companies, it recalls the responsibility of the private sector to respect human rights, and specifically calls on them to inform users about company policies that may impact their right to privacy.

The resolution notes that violations and abuses of the right to privacy increasingly affect individuals and have particular effects on women, children and vulnerable or marginalized communities. It links the right to privacy with the exercise of freedom of expression, as well as participation in political, economic, social, and cultural life, a framing that challenges increasing identification of security and surveillance by governments and corporations.

Since the UN General Assembly's first resolution on this issue in 2013, in reaction to the Snowden revelations, its approach has evolved from a largely political response to mass surveillance to addressing more complex challenges around data collection and the role of the private sector. These are encouraging developments, and have already brought about some positive change, including the establishment of a UN Special Rapporteur on the right to privacy. But more work is needed to implement the resolutions, especially the calls on states to improve their laws and practices with respect to their surveillance practices. Like all UNGA resolutions, this is non-binding and unless states take their commitments seriously and civil society applies pressure, there is a risk that these resolutions remain just words on paper.

Looking forward, the resolution suggests that the Human Rights Council (HRC) consider holding an expert workshop as a contribution to a future report of the UN High Commissioner on Human Rights on this matter. Practically speaking, this means the issue is bounced back to the HRC in Geneva, which will decide when and under what terms to hold the workshop. Expert workshops can be an excellent way to discuss challenging and complex issues outside the highly politicized confines of UNGA or the HRC, so should this workshop happen, it has the potential to be a valuable opportunity to work through some of the thorny issues around privacy in the digital age, of which there is no shortage.

1. Does the UN resolution on privacy have the power to change the laws of nations?

2. Why does the UN specifically address the role of the private sector when discussing privacy rights?

EXCERPT FROM "PRIVACY MATTERS," BY TIMOTHY PILGRIM, FROM THE OFFICE OF THE AUSTRALIAN INFORMATION COMMISSIONER, MAY 8, 2014

Presentation by Timothy Pilgrim, Privacy Commissioner, to the 'Privacy matters' public lecture at Griffith University, Brisbane, 8 May.

INTRODUCTION

It's a pleasure to be here to talk to you this morning about some of the changes to the Privacy Act that came in on 12 March, but also to talk to you about privacy awareness more generally.

It is probably worth starting today by asking 'why is privacy important?' Of course, the answer is complex, contextual and like the concept of privacy itself, ever changing.

Of course, identity security is one of the key answers to this question — in a technological and information age, issues like identity fraud and theft are an increasing problem. With the sheer volume of personal information that is stored electronically these days, protecting your privacy in the online environment is both necessary and just common sense. But there is also a larger point about the importance of privacy.

One answer to the question is that people need private space, and they need privacy to be free:

- to behave and to associate with others without the threat of constant surveillance

- to innovate, and to think, argue and act — the ingredients of any healthy democracy. [1]

One of the purposes of the Privacy Act is to support and maintain Australia's obligations to the International Covenant on Civil and Political Rights, where article 17 says:

1. No one shall be subjected to arbitrary or unlawful interference with his privacy, family, home or correspondence, nor to unlawful attacks on his honor and reputation.

2. Everyone has the right to the protection of the law against such interference or attacks.

Privacy is a human right, the Privacy Act seeks to protect it, but the right to privacy is also balanced against other competing rights, like freedom of expression, which creates a complex relationship between privacy and the media. Law enforcement and national security are other factors that need to be taken into account and balanced against the right to privacy. Different groups of people will have different opinions on how these should sit in relation to each other, and what this balance should be, which is something that is receiving a lot of media and public attention at the moment.

However, a fundamental point is that people have the right to make choices and to exercise some control about their privacy, about how their identity is used and disclosed. Privacy is about protecting information about who we are, what we do, what we think, what we believe. It is important that organisations and the Government support people's right to make the choices that work for them.

THE SCOPE OF THE PRIVACY ACT

But it is important to note that the Privacy Act is not a catch-all — it doesn't cover the acts of individuals or many small businesses, and there are a lot of areas commonly associated with privacy that are not a part of privacy legislation. Surveillance, for example, is covered by a different set of laws. However, the concept of privacy applies to a large range of issues, and how you have the right to make choices about your privacy that work for you.

New technology and privacy are increasingly connected, and more complex interactions and questions are coming up every day.

In the last year, our office has been involved in a lot of discussions about new technology and the privacy implications.

An example is that I recently provided a briefing to a Senate committee about the privacy implications of drones. Drones are a privacy issue that is quickly coming to the fore, but the issue is complicated by the fact that they can easily be owned and operated by individuals, which is not covered by the requirements of the Privacy Act.

While such technology captures the community's attention it also captures the attention of privacy regulators globally. During the year privacy regulators around the world continued to foster greater international cooperation in the light of such developments. Through forums such as the Global Privacy Enforcement Network, the APEC Cross Border Privacy Enforcement Arrangement and regional groupings of Privacy Regulators such as the Asia Pacific Privacy Authorities Forum, concerted efforts were undertaken to build a coordinated approach to regulating the protection of personal information.

During the last year we joined with privacy regulators from around the world to engage with Google about the potential privacy concerns around the development and use of Google Glass. We also participated in the Global Privacy Enforcement Network internet sweep, where regulators from around the world chose one week to target and assess the privacy policies on high traffic websites and mobile apps.

During this sweep we looked at the 50 most trafficked websites in Australia and found that most of them had issues with the readability, findability, relevance and length of their privacy policies. We will be participating in the sweep again this year — it will be taking place next week, and we will be looking at key mobile apps. With the changes to the requirements for privacy policies due to law reform, we are hoping to see an improvement in the quality of privacy policies.

The key thing to note about privacy legislation in Australia is that the Privacy Act covers information privacy, and specifically regulates the handling of 'personal information'.

Personal information is information, whether true or not, that identifies, or could reasonably identify you. This includes things like name, date of birth and address, but it also includes things like opinions and photos.

The federal Privacy Act is technology neutral principles-based legislation that came into force in the federal public sector in 1989, and extended to include parts of the private sector in 2000. Unlike other legislation, the Privacy Act is generally not prescriptive, dictating specific processes, but instead sets out a series of privacy principles that organizations must comply with in regards to the way they handle personal information.

Although the legislation is technology neutral, 25 years is a long time, especially when you consider how quickly technology has changed in the last 5 to 10 years, and continues to change. The recent reforms to the Privacy Act that came into effect on 12 March aim to take into account the way that this has impact on information handling and management, with changes to rules around transparency, information security, cross-border disclosure and direct marketing.

Part of the changes include the replacement of the two separate privacy principles for the public and private sectors with a single set that are consistent across all organizations that are covered by the Act — the Australian Privacy Principles (or APPs).

Law reform also introduces some significant changes to credit reporting rules as well as stronger enforcement powers for our office. We are now able to issue enforceable undertakings, even for issues we have investigated on our own initiative. An enforceable undertaking can require an entity to take, or to stop, a certain action or process. We are also able to issue fines of up to 1.7 million dollars for serious or repeated breaches of privacy.

LAW REFORM

There are a lot of changes to process for businesses and government due to the APPs, and a lot of those will have a direct impact on you as consumers of services. There are a few key new areas for individuals that can be drawn out of the changes.

OPENNESS

The first is openness. Under the new laws, businesses and government agencies that are covered by the Privacy Act have greater responsibility to manage information in an open and transparent way.

They must have a clearly expressed and up-to-date privacy policy explaining what they are going to do with your personal information. This policy must explain the kinds of personal information they collect and use, what they are going to do with it, and whether they are likely to disclose it overseas. They must also say how you can access and correct your personal information and make a privacy complaint.

They should also give you a 'privacy notice' when they collect your personal information, which will give you more specific information about why they are collecting your information and what they are going to do with it.

The Community attitudes to privacy survey that we ran last year shows that 55% of young people don't read the privacy policies on websites. I strongly encourage you not to be one of those people — a good privacy policy will tell you a lot that you need to know about what will happen to your personal information. We have just released a poster, which is available on our website, that will give you some practical tips of what to look for in a privacy policy, and I strongly encourage you to read it.

YOUR IDENTITY

The second key issue is about your identity. You now have the right to deal with any organization that is covered by the Privacy Act, whether public or private sector, anonymously or using a pseudonym. Obviously, there are some circumstances where this will not be appropriate, and you will have to prove your identity, but this option exists for all people in a lot of situations.

DIRECT MARKETING

The third area that is likely to impact on you as individuals in is regards to direct marketing. Organizations are only allowed to use or share your personal information for direct marketing in very specific circumstances. They must also provide you with a simple method of opting out of receiving direct marketing, and to tell you where they got your information from if you ask them.

DISCLOSING PERSONAL INFORMATION OVERSEAS

The forth significant area of change in is cross-border disclosure, where your personal information is disclosed to an organization outside of Australia. Under the APPs, if your personal information is disclosed overseas, the Australian entity remains responsible for how it is handled. There are some exceptions to this, such as when you specifically consent to it being disclosed overseas, but overall this new requirement puts a higher onus of responsibility on entities who disclose your personal information.

ACCESS AND CORRECTION

The last area that is substantially affected by the APPs is your right to access your personal information and have it corrected if necessary. Generally speaking, if you ask an entity for access to your personal information they have to provide it within a reasonable period of time, which our office considers to be within 30 days.

If the information they hold about you is incorrect, you can request and gain a correction. Again, this must take place within a reasonable period of time.

If an entity refuses to give you access or to correct your personal information, they must give you written notice outlining the reasons for their refusal.

CREDIT REPORTING

The credit reporting system is also an area that has changed significantly under law reform. The ability to get credit is something people often take for granted, but if something goes wrong it's usually at the worst possible time.

Some aspects remain the same, and some are different, but the key things to remember are:

- You have the right to access and request corrections to the information held about you by credit reporting bodies and credit providers like banks.
- In some cases if you are more than 14 days late on a bill, this information may be added to your credit report — this is your repayment history. This is NOT the same as a default.

- If you are more than 60 days late on a bill, this is a default. If the credit provider has followed a certain procedure it may be recorded on your credit report.
- A default cannot be recorded for an amount that is less than $150, or if you are under 18.
- A 'credit repair' agency cannot get information that is correct removed from your credit report.
- If there is incorrect information in your credit report, you can directly request a correction — you do not need to use a 'credit repair' agency for this.

AWARENESS

I'd like to finish up today by talking about some current issues in privacy, as well as about community aware-ness. In the age of big data, social media and cloud computing, it is increasingly important that people think about the concept of privacy and what it means to them. I am concerned that people aren't consider-ing the potential risks of disclosing too much personal information, particularly when engaging online.

I spoke briefly before about online identity secu-rity — one of the issues closely associated with this is managing your digital identity. Your digital identity is made up of a thousand tiny pieces of information that is available about you online, whether on professional networking sites like LinkedIn, in publicly available photos, in social media posts and in information about you that is shared by other people. This information can be added up to form a comprehensive and identifiable profile of you that may be used by anyone from prospective employers to direct marketing organizations. Your digital identity is real and it is almost impossible to change, so you need to consider how you want to be seen, now and into the future.

The Community attitudes to privacy survey showed that young people consider online services, including social media, to be the biggest privacy risk we face today. 60% of respondents aged 18–25 were of this opinion, but despite this, 33% of them have regretted something that they posted on social media. It is also worth noting that only 9% of Australians consider the social media industry to be trustworthy.

Australians are increasingly conscious of privacy issues – 82% of people said they knew of the existence of federal privacy laws, and 33% of Australians said that they had a problem with the way their personal information was handled in the last year. This is supported by the ever increasing number of privacy enquiries and complaints that we receive. In the 2012–13 financial year we received 1496 privacy complaints and 12 602 privacy enquiries. Already, in the current year so far we have received about **3000 complaints** and **12,000** privacy enquiries.

Our office is also receiving an increasing number of voluntary data breach notifications — this might not seem like a good thing, but the previously low numbers of data breach notifications probably indicated a failure to report them, rather than a lower number of data breaches.

Australians are consistently in support of a greater level of transparency from both government agencies and businesses when it comes to information handling — 95% of people believe that they should be informed how their information is handled and protected, and 96% of people believe that they should be informed if their personal information is lost.

[…]

CONCLUSION

Privacy is about respect for the protection of all of our personal information. That is information that says who we are, what we think, believe, feel, what we have done and what we want to do. It is about respecting the dignity of individuals.

Other people and organizations make decisions about us based on what they think they know about us through this information. That impacts each of us as we go about our daily lives. Privacy is a complex issues but the aim of privacy law is to help us set the boundaries and expectations initially through transparency of business practices to build awareness and through that trust. This should allow businesses and government to go about their legitimate activities while the community can expect their privacy to be respected.

More and more of our everyday interactions have a potential impact on privacy and that will only continue to increase, as technological solutions to information management become more and more innovative. This in itself is not a problem, but it means that we have to become more aware and more vigilant about how our personal information is used and disclosed. Familiarity can often breed complacency, but it is up to you to control your privacy. Privacy is important, and once lost, it is almost impossible to get back.

1. How can people become more actively engaged in protecting their privacy?

2. How is digital credit reporting an issue of privacy?

EXCERPT FROM "REMARKS BY THE PRESIDENT AT THE FEDERAL TRADE COMMISSION," BY FORMER PRESIDENT BARACK OBAMA, FROM THE WHITE HOUSE ARCHIVES, JANUARY 12, 2015

THE PRESIDENT: Next week, just up the street, I will deliver the State of the Union address. And it will be a chance to talk about America's resurgence, including something we can all be proud of, which is the longest stretch of private sector job growth in American history -- 58 straight months and more than 11 million new jobs. In the speech, I'm going to focus on how we can build on that progress and help more Americans feel that resurgence in their own lives, through higher wages and rising incomes and a growing middle class.

But since I've only got two years left in this job, I tend to be impatient and I didn't want to wait for the State of the Union to start sharing my plans. So I've been traveling across the country rolling out some of the ideas that we'll be talking about, a little bit of a sneak preview.

And in the 21st century -- in this dizzying age of technology and innovation -- so much of the prosperity that we seek, so many of the jobs that we create, so much of the opportunity that's available for the next generation depends on our digital economy. It depends on our ability to search and connect and shop and do business and create and discover and learn online, in cyberspace. And as we've all been reminded over the past year, including the hack of Sony, this extraordinary interconnection creates enormous opportunities, but also creates enormous vulnerabilities for us as a nation and for our economy, and for individual families.

So this week, I'm laying out some new proposals on how we can keep seizing the possibilities of an Information Age, while protecting the security and prosperity and values that we all cherish. Today, I'm focusing on how we can better protect American consumers from identity theft and ensure our privacy, including for our children at school. And then tomorrow, at the Department of Homeland Security, I'll focus on how we can work with the private sector to better defend ourselves against cyber-attacks. And final, on Wednesday, in Iowa, I'll talk about how we can give families and communities faster, cheaper access to broadband so they can succeed in the digital economy.

But I wanted to start here, at the FTC, because every day you take the lead in making sure that Americans, their hard-earned money and their privacy are protected, especially when they go online. And these days, that's pretty much for everything: managing our bank accounts, paying our bills, handling everything from medical records to movie tickets, controlling our homes —- smart houses, from smart phones. Secret Service does not let me do that. (Laughter.) But I know other people do.

And with these benefits come risks —- major companies get hacked; America's personal information, including financial information, gets stolen. And the problem is growing, and it costs us billions of dollars. In one survey, 9 out of 10 Americans say they feel like they've lost control of their personal information. In recent breaches, more than 100 million Americans have had their personal data compromised, like credit card information. When these cyber criminals start racking up charges on your card, it can destroy your credit rating. It can turn your life upside down. It may take you months to get your finances back in order. So this is a direct threat to the economic security of American families and we've got to stop it.

If we're going to be connected, then we need to be protected. As Americans, we shouldn't have to forfeit our basic privacy when we go online to do our business. And that's why, since I took office, we've been working with the private sector to strengthen our cyber defenses. A few months ago, we launched our BuySecure initiative. The federal government and companies across the country are moving to stronger chip-and-pin technology for credit cards. Here at the FTC, you're working with credit bureaus so that victims can recover their stolen identities faster, and every day you're helping consumers with IdentityTheft.gov.

So today I'm announcing new steps to protect the identities and privacy of the American people. Let me list them for you. First, we're introducing new legislation to create a single, strong national standard so Americans know when their information has been stolen or misused. Right now, almost every state has a different law on this, and it's confusing for consumers and it's confusing for companies -- and it's costly, too, to have to comply to this patchwork of laws. Sometimes, folks don't even find out their credit card information has been stolen until they see charges on their bill, and then it's too late. So under the new standard that we're proposing, companies would have to notify consumers of a breach within 30 days. In addition, we're proposing to close loopholes in the law so we can go after more criminals who steal and sell the identities of Americans —- even when they do it overseas.

Second, I'm pleased that more banks, credit card issuers and lenders are stepping up and equipping Americans with another weapon against identity theft, and that's access to their credit scores, free of charge. This includes JPMorgan Chase, Bank of America, USAA, State Employees' Credit Union, Ally Financial. Some of them are here today. I want to thank them for their participation. This means that a majority of American adults will have free access to their credit score, which is like an early warning system telling you that you've been hit by fraud so you can deal with it fast. And we're encouraging more companies to join this effort every day.

Third, we're going to be introducing new legislation -— a Consumer Privacy Bill of Rights. Working with many of you -— from the private sector and advocacy groups -- we've identified some basic principles to both protect personal privacy and ensure that industry can keep innovating. For example, we believe that consumers have the right to decide what personal data companies collect from them and how companies use that data, that information; the right to know that your personal information collected for one purpose can't then be misused by a company for a different purpose; the right to have your information stored securely by companies that are accountable for its use. We believe that there ought to be some basic baseline protections across industries. So we're going to be introducing this legislation by the end of next month, and I hope Congress joins us to make the Consumer Privacy Bill of Rights the law of the land.

And finally, we're taking a series of actions to protect the personal information and privacy of our children. Those of us with kids know how hard this can be. Whether they are texting or tweeting, or on Facebook, or Instagram, or Vine, our children are meeting up -- and they are growing up -- in cyberspace. It is all-pervasive. And here at the FTC, you've pushed back on companies and apps that collect information on our kids without permission.

And Michelle and I are like parents everywhere -- we want to make sure that our children are being smart and safe online. That's a responsibility of ours as parents. But we need partners. And we need a structure that ensures that information is not being gathered without us as parents or the kids knowing it. We want our kids' privacy protected -— wherever they sign in or log on, including at school.

Now, the good news is we've got new educational technologies that are transforming how our children learn. You've got innovative websites and apps and tablets, digital textbooks and tutors. Students are getting lessons tailored to their unique learning needs. We want to encourage that information. And it also facilitates teachers and parents tracking student progress and grades in real-time. And all this is part of what our ConnectED initiative is about -— connecting 99 percent of American students to high-speed Internet so that we're empowering students, teachers, and parents, and giving them access to worlds they may never have had access to before.

But we've already seen some instances where some companies use educational technologies to collect student data for commercial purposes, like targeted advertising. And parents have a legitimate concern about those kinds of practices.

So, today, we're proposing the Student Digital Privacy Act. That's pretty straightforward. We're saying that data collected on students in the classroom should only be used for educational purposes -— to teach our children, not to market to our children. We want to prevent companies from selling student data to third parties for purposes other than education. We want to prevent any kind of profiling that outs certain students at a disadvantage as they go through school.

And we believe that this won't just give parents more peace of mind. We're confident that it will make sure the tools we use in the classroom will actually support the breakthrough research and innovations that we need to keep unlocking new educational technologies.

Now, we didn't have to completely reinvent the wheel on this proposal. Many states have proposed similar legislation. California just passed a landmark law. And I hope Congress joins us in this national movement to protect the privacy of our children.

We won't wait for legislation, though. The Department of Education is going to offer new tools to help schools and teachers work with tech companies to protect the privacy of students. As of today, 75 companies across the country have signed on to a Student Privacy Pledge. And among other things, they're committing not to sell student information or use educational technologies to engage in targeted advertising to students.

Some of those companies are here today. We want to thank you for your leadership. I want to encourage every company that provides these technologies to our schools to join this effort. It's the right thing to do. And if you don't join this effort, then we intend to make sure that those schools and those parents know you haven't joined this effort.

So, this mission, protecting our information and privacy in the Information Age, this should not be a partisan issue. This should be something that unites all of us as Americans. It's one of those new challenges in our modern society that crosses the old divides— transcends politics, transcends ideology. Liberal, conservative, Democrat, Republican, everybody is online, and everybody understands the risks and vulnerabilities as well as opportunities that are presented by this new world.

Business leaders want their privacy and their children's privacy protected, just like everybody else does. Consumer and privacy advocates also want to make sure that America keeps leading the world in technology and innovation and apps. So there are some basic, common-sense, pragmatic steps that we ought to all be able to support.

And rather than being at odds, I think that much of this work actually reinforces each other. The more we do to protect consumer information and privacy, the harder it is for hackers to damage our businesses and hurt our economy. Meanwhile, the more companies strengthen their cybersecurity, the harder it is for hackers to steal consumer information and hurt American families. So we've got to all be working together in the same direction, and I'm confident if we do we'll be making progress.

We are the country that invented the Internet. And we're also the pioneers of this Information Age — the creators, the designers, the innovators. Our children are leaving us in the dust, if you haven't noticed. (Laughter.) They're connecting and they're collaborating like never before, and imagining a future we can only dream of. When we Americans put our minds together and our shoulder to the wheel, there's nothing we can't do. So I'm confident, if we keep at this, we can deliver the prosperity and security and privacy that all Americans deserve.

We pioneered the Internet, but we also pioneered the Bill of Rights, and a sense that each of us as individuals have a sphere of privacy around us that should not be breached, whether by our government, but also by commercial interests. And since we're pioneers in both these areas, I'm confident that we can be pioneers in crafting the kind of architecture that will allow us to both grow, innovate, and preserve those values that are so precious to us as Americans.

Thank you very much. And thanks to the FTC — (applause) — for all the great work you do to protect the American people. Thank you. (Applause.)

1. Why is it important to have a national standard when it comes to identity theft laws?

2. How does having free access to credit scores protect against identity theft?

"PRIVACY CONCEPTS: US V. EU," BY CHRISTIAN LAUX, FROM THE CENTER FOR INTERNET AND SOCIETY AT STANFORD LAW SCHOOL, SEPTEMBER 21, 2007

When it comes to Privacy Law, Europe and the U.S. are not on the same page. What is the problem? This is not the place to give an extensive answer, but here is what I think the difference boils down to:

Under the European Data Protection directives, the user (the "data subject") owns a set of legal rights entitling him to control data that are describing him, regardless of who had access to the data. Contrary to this, in the U.S. legal system, he who has rightful access to data "owns" the data and may make use of such data; such use may be limited, too, but the reasons for such limitation rely on different grounds than in the European Union.

In the European Union, a user basically has the right to be informed about how data is used (**notice requirement**), and to prevent any use he does not agree to (**consent requirement**). In short, and a bit simplified: Without consent use is forbidden. In essence, this mechanism resembles to any other Intellectual Property rights (such as Copyright, Patent and Trademark rights).

The U.S. do not have a framework similar to the European one. As a general rule, whoever has unrestricted access to data "owns" it and may use the data to the extent as such use is not forbidden. The main reasons why use could be forbidden, are

(1) the user gives **restricted access** only. As an example, before conveying data he makes the recipient

agree to use the data only for a limited purpose. Typically, a company gives such commitment in its privacy policy. If the user and a Company "agree" on a later opt-out right, this means that the user shall be able to say "no" later, instead of at the very beginning of the contact.

(2) **statute**: a company does not meet some specific duties established by a statute (such statutes may be The Gramm-Leach-Bliley Act, CAN-SPAM, or others) or

(3) **access** to data was unlawful.

For that mechanism to work, a **privacy statement** plays a very important role in the U.S. The privacy statement must properly describe the privacy practices, otherwise the company may be found to engage in unfair competition. However, in the U.S., it seems not to be necessary that a user actually agrees to a company's privacy practices. As long as the user does not object at the time of collection, the company should be fine (if it also is in compliance with any additional requirements established by statutes).

Contrary to this, a company subject to European data protection law needs to bother ways more about how to get the consent necessary to collect and use data.

1. How do American and European laws of data ownership differ?

2. Should users be able to restrict access to their data?

EXCERPT FROM "ON SOCIAL MEDIA, HOW CAN DHS TELL WHO'S AN IMMIGRANT?," BY RIANA PFEFFERKORN, FROM THE CENTER FOR INTERNET AND SOCIETY AT STANFORD LAW SCHOOL, SEPTEMBER 29, 2017

On September 18, the Department of Homeland Security (DHS) revealed a new policy for collecting immigrants' social media information. According to a Notice published in the Federal Register, effective October 18, DHS is expanding its categories of records that "constitute the official record of an individual's immigration history" to include "social media handles, aliases, associated identifiable information, and search results." In addition, the sources from which DHS creates immigration-history records will be expanded to include, among others, "publicly available information obtained from the internet," "commercial data providers" (also called "commercial data aggregators"), and "information obtained and disclosed pursuant to information sharing agreements."

DHS characterized this Notice as an administrative formality, given that the agency "has and continues to monitor publicly-available social media to protect the homeland." Indeed, this is not DHS's first rodeo when it comes to monitoring non-citizens' social media. But existing screening programs (such as those at Customs and Border Protection and the State Department), as well as a border surveillance bill now pending in the Senate, have focused on visa applicants and temporary visitors to the U.S. As noted in BuzzFeed News, which first reported on the Notice, DHS's policy will cover not just new immigrants, but also legal permanent residents (LPRs, i.e., green-card holders) and naturalized citizens. (I'm using the term "immigrants" loosely here, to include all of these categories.) That means DHS could monitor immigrants' social media long after they've settled in the U.S., not just while initially evaluating whether to admit them to the country.

So: how does DHS figure out which accounts on Facebook, Twitter, Instagram, and other services belong to existing or would-be immigrants to the U.S., rather than natural-born U.S. citizens? (That is, assuming the agency cares if you fall into the latter category, which isn't necessarily so.) Anonymous and pseudonymous accounts abound on these services. Many people share the same first and last names, so even a real name attached to an account might need disambiguation. Further, demanding that immigrants disclose their social media handles might yield under-inclusive results. Many people have multiple accounts: an "official" account, meant to be seen by parents, potential employers, and the like; and another, more secretive account kept separate from one's "real" identity. If DHS was monitoring social media even before making this official change, then it must be dealing with this issue already.

One possible avenue for determining whether a social media user is an immigrant is to demand information on the user from the platform. With a subpoena or court order, DHS can get basic subscriber information about a particular account, such as the email or IP address(es) associated with an account. The agency can then check whether the email address is associated with an individual in DHS's systems. Given an IP address, it could determine which ISP owns that IP address, then serve another subpoena or court order on the ISP to learn the subscriber's name and address, and, again, search its own systems for a match.

It's not clear from the Notice, though, that user-data demands to platforms fall among the "record source categories" available to DHS as a routine matter. Plus, there must be some grounds for legal process to issue, and compliance is not guaranteed. What if there's no specific investigation or proceeding to justify a subpoena or get a judge to sign off on a court order? What if, when served with the demand, the company does not hand over the requested account information? Twitter and Facebook both receive numerous requests every year from the federal government for basic subscriber information, and typically they provide it. However, they sometimes fight back to protect their users' anonymity, as Twitter did against an administrative summons from DHS earlier this year (prompting the agency to swiftly withdraw the summons).

This is where the newly expanded sources of records come in. Gizmodo noted that "information sharing agreements" could include surveillance agreements among the Five Eyes countries (the U.S., Canada, the U.K., Australia, and New Zealand), or DHS's agreements with private companies in the Internet and communications sectors.

The "commercial data providers" category is also unsettling. Data brokers collect and sell information about you, which they gather from public, governmental, and commercial sources. As a 2014 FTC report on data brokers notes, a data broker's dossier on an individual might identify her social media accounts. It might also include country of origin, or proxies for it: data points such as ethnicity, language, and religion from which DHS could draw an inference (however inaccurate or biased) about the individual's citizenship. (Edited to add: Of the nine brokers the FTC report studied, DHS currently contracts with two: Corelogic and Recorded Future. That's in addition to other major data brokers such as LexisNexis, credit bureaus like Equifax and TransUnion, and various background-check companies, among many others.) Of course, these dossiers aren't necessarily accurate. The risk of false positives and false negatives makes DHS's use of "commercial data providers" for immigration record purposes even more troubling.

Social media companies have acted to stop data-mining entities such as Geofeedia and Dataminr from enabling government surveillance of their users. Yet as long as they continue to sell their users' information to third-party companies (for purposes such as advertising and analytics), they have little effective control over where it ultimately ends up. Once it goes out the door, user data can get re-sold and combined with other information by a constellation of data-mining companies. Cutting off Geofeedia and Dataminr means that government agencies will simply switch to other monitoring companies that are ready, willing, and able to provide the information they need, whether directly or through layers of intermediaries.

Finally, it may be that for all the massive amounts of data they hold about us, existing data aggregators cannot meet DHS's information needs. After all, over 43 million people in the U.S. are foreign-born. (That includes over 13 million LPRs and over 7 million citizens who were naturalized in the last decade alone.) But DHS need not worry: companies such as IBM are lining up for the opportunity to develop data-mining software for "extreme vetting" of visitors to the U.S. That software could be repurposed, or new software developed, to monitor immigrants living in the U.S. as well as temporary visitors to our country.

This blog post thought through some of the ways DHS might try to tell immigrants apart from natural-born American citizens on social media. Suspicionless mass monitoring of immigrants via social media is surely a complicated logistical challenge. It's also privacy-invasive, speech-chilling, and un-American.

[…]

1. Why could the DHS's use of "commercial data providers" be seen as problematic?

2. Should social media sites protect immigrants' privacy from government agencies?

"UK PRIVACY LAWS MAY ALLOW 230 MILLION AMERICANS TO DEMAND PERSONALITY PROFILES CREATED BY TRUMP'S BIG DATA ALLY," BY GLYN MOODY, FROM *PRIVACY NEWS ONLINE*, OCTOBER 4, 2017

Earlier this week, Facebook released a statement about ads it carried which had been paid for by Russian sources. It now says that around ten million people in the US saw the ads, and that 44% of total ad impressions were before the 2016 US election. Strikingly, for 50% of the ads less than $3 was spent. This suggests that many of the ads were micro-targeted. A recent article in the *Washington Post* confirms the precision of the operation:

> "Russian operatives set up an array of misleading Web sites and social media pages to identify American voters susceptible to propaganda, then used a powerful Facebook tool to repeatedly send them messages designed to influence their political behavior, say people familiar with the investigation into foreign meddling in the U.S. election."

However, there is increasing evidence that an even more sophisticated approach was used to influence voters in the US election, and on a far larger scale, by the little-known company Cambridge Analytica. The company certainly played a key role there, as its Web site proclaims:

> "Cambridge Analytica provided the Donald J. Trump for President campaign with the expertise and insights that helped win the White House, causing the most remarkable victory in modern U.S. political history."

Perhaps the best exploration of Cambridge Analytica and its methods is an article originally published in German last year, and available in English on *Motherboard*. It describes the field of psychometrics, which seeks to measure psychological traits. The "OCEAN" model uses five axes to do this: those of openness, conscientiousness, extroversion, agreeableness, and neuroticism.

An otherwise rather obscure field was revolutionized by the work of the researcher Michal Kosinski. He had the idea of creating a Facebook app called "MyPersonality" to evaluate the OCEAN profile of online respondents. Millions of people took the test, creating the largest dataset of psychometric scores along with associated Facebook profiles ever to be collected. Kosinki then looked for correlations between the profiles and the kind of things respondents had liked on Facebook – information that was publicly available at the time. Soon he found he was able to predict a subject's answers to the OCEAN questions just by looking at fewer than a hundred of his or her likes. But the biggest breakthrough came from realizing that things worked the other way too:

> "not only can psychological profiles be created from your data, but your data can also be used the other way round to search for specific profiles: all anxious fathers, all angry introverts, for example – or maybe even all undecided Democrats? Essentially, what Kosinski had invented was sort of a people search engine."

Cambridge Analytica encourages visitors to its Web site to evaluate themselves using the OCEAN psychometric framework. By applying these kind of technique to huge quantities of personal data obtained from many different sources, both online and offline, Cambridge Analytica has taken this approach to its ultimate conclusion. It has built up detailed profiles of US voters, as it proudly boasts: "With up to 5,000 data points on over 230 million American voters, we build your custom target audience, then use this crucial information to engage, persuade, and motivate them to act."

Although still relatively unknown, Cambridge Analytica turns out to have extremely close links with some of the most powerful people in Western politics. A long article in the *Guardian* earlier this year attempted to disentangle the complicated relationships between Donald Trump, his billionaire backer Robert Mercer, Steve Bannon and Cambridge Analytica, as well as other key players. It also explores the involvement of the company with the Brexit referendum that saw a slim majority of people in the UK vote to leave the European Union. As a now-deleted statement from the Leave.eu campaign explained in November 2015:

> "Cambridge Analytica are world leaders in target voter messaging. They will be helping us map the British electorate and what they believe in, enabling us to better engage with voters. Most elections are fought using demographic and socio-economic data. Cambridge Analytica's psychographic methodology however is on another level of sophistication."

The UK's data privacy watchdog, the Information Commissioner's Office, is currently investigating how voters were targeted during the Brexit referendum campaign. The *Guardian* reports the Commissioner as saying: "if political campaigns or third-party companies are able to gather up very precise digital trails to then individually target people, that is an area [where] they are going to be outside the law".

The fact that Cambridge Analytica was involved with two of the biggest political upsets in recent political history – the election of Donald Trump and the Brexit vote – is intriguing. It turns out that there's another British connection, one which may open the way for those 230 million US voters to find out what exactly Cambridge Analytica holds on them:

"although Cambridge Analytica is largely owned by Trump's biggest donor, hedge-fund billionaire Robert Mercer, and though its vice-president at the time of the US election was Trump's former chief strategist, Steve Bannon, the company was spun out of an older British military and elections contractor, SCL, with which it still shares staff, directors and a London office."

As the *Guardian* explains, because Cambridge Analytica seems to have processed Americans' data in Britain, under UK data protection laws US citizens can demand to see that information. And that is precisely what the US professor David Carroll is doing, using crowd-funding to support his legal action. If he is successful, it will be a simple matter for all US voters to follow his example, and to demand information about the thousands of data points that Cambridge Analytica claims it holds about them.

Carroll isn't the only person trying to shine light on the activities of companies gathering personal data on a huge scale. Paul-Olivier Dehaye wants to do something similar for Facebook. He has asked the company for details about what it holds on him. He's published his formal request to the company, and has set up an easy-to-use site that helps other Facebook users do the same.

It's increasingly clear that well-known Internet companies like Facebook, as well as secretive outfits like Cambridge Analytica, can have a big impact on our lives in important ways. Applying their algorithmic engines to the vast databases filled with intimate details of our personal interests and activities, decisions are made about us, and actions taken as a result, without us knowing how or why. As we've written before, the time has come to bring some accountability to algorithmic decision-making. In the wake of revelations about Russian-funded ads on Facebook, it looks like politicians are starting to agree.

1. Should social media sites be transparent about what data they keep and distribute for each user?

2. Should political ads be able to target specific individuals? Why or why not?

CHAPTER 3

WHAT THE COURTS SAY

While it's the government's job to protect citizens' privacy against foreign threats, it is up to the courts to protect the privacy of citizens from their government. It is easy to see that our laws have not kept up with the advances of technology. It is through laws that we can better protect citizens and guide tech companies towards methods that protect privacy. Currently the law is very clear about the ways the state can search the physical property of citizens, but when it comes to digital property the laws are still unclear. It is up to the courts now to decide if the Fourth Amendment protects things like citizens' cell phone passwords or social media records. Courts have the important job of interpreting how existing laws apply to new technology. The following articles will show how the courts are navigating the legality of privacy.

"HOW PRIVACY LAW AFFECTS MEDICAL AND SCIENTIFIC RESEARCH," BY JOHN CONLEY, FROM *GENOMICS LAW REPORT*, SEPTEMBER 1, 2015

Over the last five or so years my law practice has focused increasingly on privacy law, both domestic and international. In hindsight, this was a predictable outcome: as an intellectual property [IP] lawyer, many of my clients do business on the Internet or are engaged in scientific research and development, with many of the latter in the health care area. These are the very kinds of people who need to worry about privacy—of their customers, users, patients, and subjects. As they started on focusing on privacy concerns, these clients turned to their IP lawyers for help, and my Robinson Bradshaw colleagues and I have tried to stay ahead of their needs.

As a consequence of my growing privacy practice, I am regularly called on to give overviews to other lawyers as well as non-lawyers in the scientific and business communities. I thought it might be useful to devote a GLR post to a privacy law summary targeted at readers who conduct medical and other scientific research. Privacy law is a transnational mess, so this will be a bit longer than I'd like—my apologies, and please don't shoot the messenger—but I'll try to cut through the legal jargon.

SOURCES OF MODERN PRIVACY LAW

In the United States, there is no general federal privacy law yet. Federal laws are sector-specific, covering such areas

as health (HIPAA), finance, and online businesses that
target children. In addition, the Federal Trade Commission is
beginning to assert itself as a general regulator of privacy.
There are also some federal criminal laws and principles
that have privacy implications (anti-wiretapping laws and
protections against unreasonable searches, for instances),
but these are beyond the scope of this discussion.

In the absence of a comprehensive federal privacy
law, the states are the most important source of general
privacy law. California has long been the leader, and remains
so. Hence one piece of advice I always give to clients: comply
with California law and you'll be 99% safe everywhere.

The development of international privacy law has
been driven by the European Union, with other countries
(except the U.S.) following its lead and adopting EU-style
laws. The EU approach is fundamentally different from
that taken in this country. The development of U.S. privacy
statutes, both state and federal, has largely been driven
by a concern with the financial consequences of identity
theft. Thus, most American laws protect "personally identifiable information," usually defined as a name, social
security number, or the like, that is linked to an account
number or other financial identifier. In Europe, by contrast,
privacy is treated as a fundamental human right—what
Americans would think of as a constitutional right. This
is understandable, since there are millions of people in
Europe with a living memory of storm troopers or secret
police knocking on doors in the middle of the night and
dragging people away. Consequently, EU privacy law is
generally far more protective than American, protecting
any kind of personal information, prohibiting any kind of
intrusion on privacy or seclusion, and putting a much

greater burden of compliance on businesses and other private actors (but not always on governments—think of the ubiquitous surveillance cameras that saturate the United Kingdom).

FOUR WAVES OF U.S. STATE PRIVACY LAWS

State privacy laws have come in what privacy experts refer to as "four waves." The first, toward the end of the last century, consisted of antihacking laws, both criminal and civil. The second or "reactive" wave, led by a 2003 California law, required notification to potential victims of data security breaches. The third, "proactive" wave, again stimulated by California legislation, requires that entities holding personally identifiable information use "reasonable security procedures and practices." The fourth wave of state laws, which are just beginning to be enacted, require such specific security measures as encryption and physical and technical controls. A parallel development is that California and other states are moving into the health sector with privacy requirements that may be more onerous than those imposed by HIPAA.

It is important to emphasize two things about these state laws. First, unless specifically displaced ("preempted," in legal terms) by a federal law like HIPAA, you should assume that they will apply to medical and other scientific research unless they are specifically displaced. Second, they usually apply to all kinds of data storage, from paper records to the cloud. In fact, there is little privacy law anywhere that relates specifically to the cloud, so cloud-using researchers must try to adapt the existing rules to that environment.

FTC REGULATION

Under the New Deal-era Federal Trade Commission
Act, the FTC has broad jurisdiction to prohibit and prevent "unfair or deceptive acts or practices." The FTC
has jurisdiction over all for-profit companies involved in
interstate commerce, but not non-profits—a significant
distinction for many research entities. Until the last few
years, the FTC's approach to privacy was simple: if you
have an announced privacy policy, make sure you live up
to it. More recently, however the FTC has begun to create
and enforce substantive standards for privacy policies
and practices, setting itself up as an all-purpose federal
privacy regulator. The new initiative focuses on "privacy
by design," including "reasonable efforts" in data security, data retention and disposal, and data accuracy. The
FTC's authority to enforce these standards was recently
upheld by a federal appellate court in a case called
Wyndham Hotels.

The FTC has promised a collaborative, "soft-law"
(best practices rather than rules) approach, but there
are skeptics (including me). The FTC issued a Privacy
Framework report in March 2013 that fills in many details
of its evolving standards and regulatory plans. Even
though many research organizations are not subject to
the FTC's jurisdiction, it would be prudent to assume that
other regulators will look to the Privacy Framework for
guidance in developing their own standards. Accordingly, it would make sense to treat the FTC framework
as, at a minimum, a set of best practices to consult in
shaping your organization's privacy program.

HIPAA

HIPAA restricts unauthorized use of personally identifiable health information to care-related activities by providers and their "business associates." However, unauthorized research use or disclosure is permitted, as long as they are approved by an Institutional Review Board. De-identified health data are generally not restricted. Overall, HIPAA requires "reasonable and appropriate administrative, technical, and physical safeguards" in the handling of health data. These rules should apply to cloud computing, and Cloud Service Providers are probably business associates covered by HIPAA.

INTERNATIONAL LAW: THE EU APPROACH

The EU is currently operating under its 1995 Data Protection Directive. A Directive is a detailed standard that individual member countries must adopt through national legislation, a process that inevitably produces country-by-country variation. Thus, compliance currently requires familiarity with both the directive and the national laws of the particular countries in which research data will be collected, processed, or stored. A 2012 Data Regulation (an EU-level law that takes effect automatically in all member countries) is pending, with many of its details still being debated. It seems likely to get final approval in the next several months, but we've been hearing that for more than two years now.

The core features of the 1995 Directive include the following:

- It covers all *personal data*: anything identifiable to a person.
- *Health-related* and *genetic* data are always *sensitive*, and thus subject to enhanced protection.
- The burden of compliance is on the *controller*—the party that directs *processing*, which includes collection, storage, transmission, or analysis of the data.
- *Consent of the data subject* is generally required for any processing.
- Processing must be for legitimate purposes and *proportional* to those purposes.
- The subject has rights of *access*, *objection* and *opt-out.*
- The controller must ensure the *security* and *integrity* of the data.

The 800-pound gorilla in the 1995 Directive is a set of rules concerning transferring personal data to non-EU countries. These rules clearly apply to medical and scientific research data. Transfer is generally forbidden unless the EU has certified the recipient country as providing EU-level privacy protection. The U.S. does not meet this standard. The following alternatives are available:

(1) Enter the U.S. Department of Commerce Safe Harbor, whereby a U.S company certifies that its policies and practices meet EU standards. However, the EU has sent strong signals that it may drop out of this program, and it is not available for nonprofits in any event.

(2) Use EU-approved contract terms between the data exporter and importer. The U.S. party must provide EU-level protection, "respond" to EU mediation and

"accept" the decision of a European national court—though it can contest jurisdiction, which seems a bit contradictory.

(3) Do the same thing through "binding corporate rules," through which an American company adopts the EU principles and provides mechanisms for ensuring compliance.

None of these approaches has gained much traction in this country, with American companies generally ignoring the problem.

The pending 2012 Privacy Regulation will follow similar principles but also make some significant changes. The proposed changes include the following:

- *Scope*: The Regulation protects anyone who can be reasonably identified from the data, and applies to all data processing activities by entities "offering goods or services" to people in the EU or "monitoring their behavior."
- *Remedies*: Private lawsuits can be brought in a plaintiff's national court, and the EU can impose administrative penalties up to the greater of 1 million euros or 2% of gross revenues.
- *The burden is on the controller* to prove "explicit" consent by subjects.
- *"Right to be forgotten, and to erasure"*: Under this most controversial provision, if a subject withdraws consent, the controller must render the data inaccessible, even if on the Internet. (Note, however, that last year the Court of Justice of the EU found that there is a right to be forgotten under existing law.)

Again, remember that countries around the world—with the notable exception of the U.S.—have followed the EU's lead in enacting privacy laws. Expect that most other countries, especially in the developed world, will have privacy laws that follow the principles of the 1995 EU Directive. In the future, an international move in the direction of the new Regulation can be expected.

MEDICAL AND SCIENTIFIC RESEARCH UNDER CURRENT EU LAW

All medical data, and much other scientific research data, will be characterized as "sensitive" and thus subject to the highest level of scrutiny and restriction. Since the Directive has been implemented at the national level, there is significant country-by-country variation in the rules pertaining to research—which, by the way, tend to be detailed and complex. Nonetheless, it is possible to simplify compliance for a multinational research project by creating an "establishment" in one country and centralizing the project there. Many American observers believe that the UK offers the most research-friendly environment in which to set up an establishment (in addition to avoiding language barriers).

Critical country-by-country regulatory variables include: whether the approval of the national Data Protection Authority is required before collecting data; whether individual subject consent is necessary and, if so, is sufficient in order to collect or export particular kinds of data; and whether de-identified or anonymized data is exempt from regulation.

THE EFFECT OF THE PROPOSED DATA REGULATION

The original draft of the Regulation had a number of fairly clear research exemptions. However, there is in ongoing debate about the final version among the EU Parliament, an expert group called the Article 29 Working Party, and innumerable research and privacy advocates—people we Americans would call lobbyists. The issues being debated include the status of "pseudonymous" data (de-identification and anonymization don't appear to be taken seriously as a technical matter) and the nature of subject consent that will be required for research. Like everything else with the Regulation, the final outcome remains uncertain.

NON-GOVERNMENTAL INITIATIVES

In what might be the most significant recent development in the non-governmental arena, in October 2014 the International Standards Organization published best a practices code for cloud computing. Rather than specifying outcomes, it focuses on architecture and processes. Not surprisingly, given the EU's dominance in international privacy law, the code has been EU-driven and is EU-like. Although these best practices are not law, they could well be read into legal definitions of "reasonableness" imposed by courts and agencies. Microsoft adopted the standards in February 2015.

SUMMARY: FIVE KEYS TO COMPLIANCE

On a practical level, researchers should focus on these five keys to compliance with these various state, federal, and international laws:

- Comply with California law and you'll usually be in compliance with other states' laws.
- Comply with relevant federal sector law—in most research contexts, it will be HIPAA.
- Watch out for the FTC—even if you're a non-profit, the FTC's standards may have influence.
- Outside the U.S., comply with EU law—but it's changing.
- Assume that all of this applies to the cloud, and will apply to future storage and processing environments.

1. What is the right to be forgotten?

2. Why do medical researchers have to protect patients' privacy?

"ALASKA DEFTLY BALANCES PRIVACY RIGHTS AND PUBLIC INTEREST," BY DAVID MORRIS, FROM *ON THE COMMONS*, DECEMBER 9, 2014

SMART POLICIES ON MARIJUANA, ALCOHOL AND DRUGS SHOULD BE MODEL FOR US SUPREME COURT

Politicians left and right often use pet phrases to justify their positions: states rights, individual liberty, personal responsibility. Rarely are these consistently applied.

Even more rarely do politicians or political parties offer a coherent framework for deciding when a higher level of government should preempt a lower level of government or when individual liberty trumps state regulation. Which makes what has happened in Alaska so refreshing and instructive. The issue addressed was the right of individuals to use drugs when the state outlaws their use.

In August 1972, a little more than 13 years after Alaska became a state, its citizens voted overwhelmingly (86-14%) to add a two-sentence amendment to their state Constitution. "The right of the people to privacy is recognized and shall not be infringed. The legislature shall implement this section."

In 1972 being caught in possession of marijuana got you the equivalent of a traffic ticket in Alaska. When attorney Irwin Ravin refused to sign his traffic ticket he was arrested. The case went to the Alaska Supreme Court. In 1975 the Court held that Alaska's new Constitutional right to privacy protected an adult's right to use marijuana in the home.

The Constitutional provision led the Court to set a high burden of proof for the state to justify its invasion of Ravin's privacy: "Where there is a significant encroachment upon personal liberty, the State may prevail only upon showing a subordinating interest which is compelling." The Court stated that the law must be shown "necessary, and not merely rationally related, to the accomplishment of a permissible state policy."

The Court found the state had not met that standard. It had not proven that the health and safety benefits to the community outweighed the right of individual privacy when it came to using marijuana. After extensively reviewing the evidence the Court determined, "the use of marijuana, as it is presently used in the United States today, does not constitute a public health problem of any significant dimensions. It is, for instance, far more innocuous in terms of physiological and social damage than alcohol or tobacco."

Later, when Alaskans became infected with the same reefer madness as the rest of the country and imposed stiffer penalties the Alaska Supreme Court continued to rule that using marijuana in one's home was Constitutionally protected.

In 1978 the Court again examined the balance between state authority to protect the health and safety and the right to personal use of drugs. This time the drug involved was cocaine. The Court again examined the evidence but this time found cocaine a far more dangerous drug than marijuana. For example, cocaine, unlike marijuana, can cause death. In its 1978 decision the Court reaffirmed the 1972 framework that would guide its decision making, declaring "the balance [of the individual's interest in privacy and the government's interest in health and safety] requires a heavier burden on the state to sustain the legislation in light of the (privacy) right involved."

But in this case it came down on the side of the state, finding a "sufficiently close and substantial relationship" between the prohibition and the legislative purpose of protecting the general health and welfare.

In 1984 the Court again explored the tension between the state's right to protect the health and safety of its citizens and the right of the individual to be left alone. This time the drug involved was alcohol. In 1979 the Alaskan legislature had given communities the "local option" of the importation and sale of alcohol, although they could not ban its use within the home. Hugh Harrison was convicted of importing alcohol into the village of the dry community of St. Mary's. He challenged the constitutionality of the local option law, arguing, among other things that it violated his Constitutional right of privacy.

The Court disagreed, finding that alcohol was more like cocaine than marijuana, "The evidence presented at the omnibus hearing unmistakably established a correlation between alcohol consumption and poor health, death, family violence, child abuse, and crime.... Given this evidence, we conclude that the state has met its burden of justifying the local option law as a health and welfare measure."

In 1986 the local option law was amended to allow communities to ban possession of alcohol.

In November 2014, Alaskan voters overwhelmingly approved a ballot measure to legalize the possession and sale of marijuana, making the 1975 Court decision moot. But a number of Alaskan communities have asked the legislature to extend their local option to include marijuana as well as alcohol. The legislature may well delegate to them the authority to ban the import, sale and public use of marijuana within their borders. But the Court decision will prohibit communities from banning the possession or personal use of marijuana in one's home.

One might disagree with the Court's reasoning in any one of its decisions. But I trust we can all support its transparent and accessible decision-making framework and its reliance on scientific evidence to determine the balance between the right of the state to protect its citizens with the right of its citizens to be left alone. The U.S. Congress and Supreme Court have much to learn from the next to last state to join the Union.

1. Should privacy rights protect the use of non-lethal drugs in the home?

2. Why did Alaskan courts rule marijuana use was protected by privacy rights, but cocaine use was not?

"CAN CUSTOMS AND BORDER OFFICIALS SEARCH YOUR PHONE? THESE ARE YOUR RIGHTS," BY PATRICK G. LEE, FROM *PROPUBLICA*, MARCH 13, 2017

RECENT DETENTIONS AND SEIZURES OF PHONES AND OTHER MATERIAL FROM TRAVELERS TO THE UNITED STATES HAVE SPARKED ALARM. WE DETAIL WHAT POWERS CUSTOMS AND BORDER PROTECTION OFFICIALS HAVE OVER YOU AND YOUR DEVICES.

A NASA scientist heading home to the U.S. said he was detained in January at a Houston airport, where Customs and Border Protection officers pressured him for access to his work phone and its potentially sensitive contents.

Last month, CBP agents checked the identification of passengers leaving a domestic flight at New York's John F. Kennedy Airport during a search for an immigrant with a deportation order.

And in October, border agents seized phones and other work-related material from a Canadian photojournalist. They blocked him from entering the U.S. after he refused to unlock the phones, citing his obligation to protect his sources.

These and other recent incidents have revived confusion and alarm over what powers border officials actually have and, perhaps more importantly, how to know when they are overstepping their authority.

The unsettling fact is that border officials have long had broad powers — many people just don't know about them. Border officials, for instance, have search powers that extend 100 air miles inland from any external boundary of the U.S. That means border agents can stop and question people at fixed checkpoints dozens of miles from U.S. borders. They can also pull over motorists whom they suspect of a crime as part of "roving" border patrol operations.

Sowing even more uneasiness, ambiguity around the agency's search powers — especially over electronic devices — has persisted for years as courts nationwide address legal challenges raised by travelers, privacy advocates and civil-rights groups.

We've dug out answers about the current state-of-play when it comes to border searches, along with links to more detailed resources.

DOESN'T THE FOURTH AMENDMENT PROTECT US FROM "UNREASONABLE SEARCHES AND SEIZURES"?

Yes. The Fourth Amendment to the Constitution articulates the "right of the people to be secure in their persons, houses, papers, and effects, against unreasonable searches and seizures." However, those protections are lessened when entering the country at international terminals at airports, other ports of entry and subsequently any location that falls within 100 air miles of an external U.S. boundary.

HOW BROAD IS CUSTOMS AND BORDER PROTECTION'S SEARCH AUTHORITY?

According to federal statutes, regulations and court decisions, CBP officers have the authority to inspect, without a warrant, any person trying to gain entry into the country and their belongings. CBP can also question individuals about their citizenship or immigration status and ask for documents that prove admissibility into the country.

This blanket authority for warrantless, routine searches at a port of entry ends when CBP decides to undertake a more invasive procedure, such as a body cavity search. For these kinds of actions, the CBP official needs to have some level of suspicion that a particular person is engaged in illicit activity, not simply that the individual is trying to enter the U.S.

DOES CBP'S SEARCH AUTHORITY COVER ELECTRONIC DEVICES LIKE SMARTPHONES AND LAPTOPS?

Yes. CBP refers to several statutes and regulations in justifying its authority to examine "computers, disks, drives, tapes, mobile phones and other communication devices, cameras, music and other media players, and any other electronic or digital devices."

According to current CBP policy, officials should search electronic devices with a supervisor in the room, when feasible, and also in front of the person being questioned "unless there are national security, law enforcement, or other operational considerations" that take priority. For instance, if allowing a traveler to witness the search would reveal sensitive law enforcement techniques or compromise an investigation, "it may not be appropriate to allow the individual to be aware of or participate in a border search," according to a 2009 privacy impact assessment by the Department of Homeland Security.

CBP says it can conduct these searches "with or without" specific suspicion that the person who possesses the items is involved in a crime.

With a supervisor's sign-off, CBP officers can also seize an electronic device — or a copy of the information on the device — "for a brief, reasonable period of time to perform a thorough border search." Such seizures typically shouldn't exceed five days, although officers can apply for extensions in up to one-week increments, according to CBP policy. If a review of the device and its contents does not turn up probable cause for seizing it, CBP says it will destroy the copied information and return the device to its owner.

CAN CBP REALLY SEARCH MY ELECTRONIC DEVICES WITHOUT ANY SPECIFIC SUSPICION THAT I MIGHT HAVE COMMITTED A CRIME?

The Supreme Court has not directly ruled on this issue. However, a 2013 decision from the U.S. Court of Appeals for the Ninth Circuit — one level below the Supreme Court — provides some guidance on potential limits to CBP's search authority.

In a majority decision, the court affirmed that cursory searches of laptops — such as having travelers turn their devices on and then examining their contents — does not require any specific suspicions about the travelers to justify them.

The court, however, raised the bar for a "forensic examination" of the devices, such as using "computer software to analyze a hard drive." For these more powerful, intrusive and comprehensive searches, which could provide access to deleted files and search histories, password-protected information and other private details, border officials must have a "reasonable suspicion" of criminal activity — not just a hunch.

As it stands, the 2013 appeals court decision legally applies only to the nine Western states in the Ninth Circuit, including California, Arizona, Nevada, Oregon and Washington. It's not clear whether CBP has taken the 2013 decision into account more broadly: The last time the agency publicly updated its policy for searching electronic devices was in 2009. CBP is currently reviewing that policy and there is "no specific timeline" for when an updated version might be announced, according to the agency.

"Laptop computers, iPads and the like are simultaneously offices and personal diaries. They contain the most intimate details of our lives," the court's decision said. "It is little comfort to assume that the government — for now — does not have the time or resources to seize and search the millions of devices that accompany the millions of travelers who cross our borders. It is the potential unfettered dragnet effect that is troublesome."

During the 2016 fiscal year, CBP officials conducted 23,877 electronic media searches, a five-fold increase from the previous year. In both the 2015 and 2016 fiscal years, the agency processed more than 380 million arriving travelers.

AM I LEGALLY REQUIRED TO DISCLOSE THE PASSWORD FOR MY ELECTRONIC DEVICE OR SOCIAL MEDIA, IF CBP ASKS FOR IT?

That's still an unsettled question, according to Liza Goitein, co-director of the Liberty and National

Security Program at the Brennan Center for Justice. "Until it becomes clear that it's illegal to do that, they're going to continue to ask," she said.

The Fifth Amendment says that no one shall be made to serve as "a witness against himself" in a criminal case. Lower courts, however, have produced differing decisions on how exactly the Fifth Amendment applies to the disclosure of passwords to electronic devices.

Customs officers have the statutory authority "to demand the assistance of any person in making any arrest, search, or seizure authorized by any law enforced or administered by customs officers, if such assistance may be necessary." That statute has traditionally been invoked by immigration agents to enlist the help of local, state and other federal law enforcement agencies, according to Nathan Wessler, a staff attorney with the ACLU's Speech, Privacy and Technology Project. Whether the statute also compels individuals being interrogated by border officials to divulge their passwords has not been directly addressed by a court, Wessler said.

Even with this legal uncertainty, CBP officials have broad leverage to induce travelers to share password information, especially when someone just wants to catch their flight, get home to family or be allowed to enter the country. "Failure to provide information to assist CBP may result in the detention and/or seizure of the electronic device," according to a statement provided by CBP.

Travelers who refuse to give up passwords could also be detained for longer periods and have their bags searched more intrusively. Foreign visitors could be turned away at the border, and green card holders could be questioned and challenged about their continued legal status.

"People need to think about their own risks when they are deciding what to do. US citizens may be comfortable doing things that non-citizens aren't, because of how CBP may react," Wessler said.

WHAT IS SOME PRACTICAL ADVICE FOR PROTECTING MY DIGITAL INFORMATION?

Consider which devices you absolutely need to travel with, and which ones you can leave at home. Setting a strong password and encrypting your devices are helpful in protecting your data, but you may still lose access to your devices for undefined periods should border officials decide to seize and examine their contents.

Another option is to leave all of your devices behind and carry a travel-only phone free of most personal information. However, even this approach carries risks. "We also flag the reality that if you go to extreme measures to protect your data at the border, that itself may raise suspicion with border agents," according to Sophia Cope, a staff attorney at the Electronic Frontier Foundation. "It's so hard to tell what a single border agent is going to do."

DOES CBP RECOGNIZE ANY EXCEPTIONS TO WHAT IT CAN EXAMINE ON ELECTRONIC DEVICES?

If CBP officials want to search legal documents, attorney work product or information protected by attorney-client privilege, they may have to follow "special handling procedures," according to agency policy. If there's suspicion that the information includes evidence of a crime or otherwise relates to "the jurisdiction of CBP," the border official must consult the CBP associate/assistant chief counsel before undertaking the search.

As for medical records and journalists' notes, CBP says its officers will follow relevant federal laws and agency policies in handling them. When asked for more information on these procedures, an agency spokesperson said that CBP has "specific provisions" for dealing with this kind of information, but did not elaborate further. Questions that arise regarding these potentially sensitive materials can be handled by the CBP associate/assistant chief counsel, according to CBP policy. The agency also says that it will protect business or commercial information from "unauthorized disclosure."

AM I ENTITLED TO A LAWYER IF I'M DETAINED FOR FURTHER QUESTIONING BY CBP?

No. According to a statement provided by CBP, "All international travelers arriving to the U.S. are subject to CBP processing, and travelers bear the burden of proof to establish that they are clearly eligible to enter the United States. Travelers are not entitled to representation during CBP administrative processing, such as primary and secondary inspection."

Even so, some immigration lawyers recommend that travelers carry with them the number for a legal aid hotline or a specific lawyer who will be able to help them, should they get detained for further questioning at a port of entry.

"It is good practice to ask to speak to a lawyer," said Paromita Shah, associate director at the National

Immigration Project of the National Lawyers Guild. "We always encourage people to have a number where their attorney can be reached, so they can explain what is happening and their attorney can try to intervene. It's definitely true that they may not be able to get into the actual space, but they can certainly intervene."

Lawyers who fill out this form on behalf of a traveler headed into the United States might be allowed to advocate for that individual, although local practices can vary, according to Shah.

CAN I RECORD MY INTERACTION WITH CBP OFFICIALS?

Individuals on public land are allowed to record and photograph CBP operations so long as their actions do not hinder traffic, according to CBP. However, the agency prohibits recording and photography in locations with special security and privacy concerns, including some parts of international airports and other secure port areas.

DOES CBP'S POWER TO STOP AND QUESTION PEOPLE EXTEND BEYOND THE BORDER AND PORTS OF ENTRY?

Yes. Federal statutes and regulations empower CBP to conduct warrantless searches for people travelling illegally from another country in any "railway car, aircraft, conveyance, or vehicle" within 100 air miles from "any external boundary" of the country. About two-thirds of the U.S. population live in this zone, including the residents of New York City, Los Angeles, Chicago, Philadelphia and Houston, according to the ACLU.

As a result, CBP currently operates 35 checkpoints, where they can stop and question motorists traveling in the U.S. about their immigration status and make "quick observations of what is in plain view" in the vehicle without a warrant, according to the agency. Even at a checkpoint, however, border officials cannot search a vehicle's contents or its occupants unless they have probable cause of wrongdoing, the agency says. Failing that, CBP officials can ask motorists to allow them to conduct a search, but travelers are not obligated to give consent.

When asked how many people were stopped at CBP checkpoints in recent years, as well as the proportion of those individuals detained for further scrutiny, CBP said they didn't have the data "on hand" but that the number of people referred for secondary questioning was "minimum." At the same time, the agency says that checkpoints "have proven to be highly effective tools in halting the flow of illegal traffic into the United States."

Within 25 miles of any external boundary, CBP has the additional patrol power to enter onto private land, not including dwellings, without a warrant.

WHERE CAN CBP SET UP CHECKPOINTS?

CBP chooses checkpoint locations within the 100-mile zone that help "maximize border enforcement while minimizing effects on legitimate traffic," the agency says.

At airports that fall within the 100-mile zone, CBP can also set up checkpoints next to airport security to screen domestic passengers who are trying to board their flights, according to Chris Rickerd, a policy counsel at the ACLU's National Political Advocacy Department.

"When you fly out of an airport in the southwestern border, say McAllen, Brownsville or El Paso, you have Border Patrol standing beside TSA when they're doing the checks for security. They ask you the same questions as when you're at a checkpoint. 'Are you a US citizen?' They're essentially doing a brief immigration inquiry in the airport because it's part of the 100-mile zone," Rickerd said. "I haven't seen this at the northern border."

CAN CBP DO ANYTHING OUTSIDE OF THE 100-MILE ZONE?

Yes. Many of CBP's law enforcement and patrol activities, such as questioning individuals, collecting evidence and making arrests, are not subject to the 100-mile rule, the agency says. For instance, the geographical limit does not apply to stops in which border agents pull a vehicle over as part of a "roving patrol" and not a fixed checkpoint, according to Rickerd of the ACLU. In these scenarios, border agents need reasonable suspicion that an immigration violation or crime has occurred to justify the stop, Rickerd said. For stops outside the 100-mile zone, CBP agents must have probable cause of wrongdoing, the agency said.

The ACLU has sued the government multiple times for data on roving patrol and checkpoint stops. Based on an analysis of records released in response to one of those lawsuits, the ACLU found that CBP officials in Arizona failed "to record any stops that do not lead to an arrest, even when the stop results in a lengthy detention, search, and/or property damage."

The lack of detailed and easily accessible data poses a challenge to those seeking to hold CBP accountable to its duties.

"On the one hand, we fight so hard for reasonable suspicion to actually exist rather than just the whim of an officer to stop someone, but on the other hand, it's not a standard with a lot of teeth," Rickerd said. "The courts would scrutinize it to see if there's anything impermissible about what's going on. But if we don't have data, how do you figure that out?"

1. Should Customs and Border Protection (CBP) officials be allowed to ask for social media passwords?

2. Should CBP officials be required to record information about all stops made outside the 100-mile border zone?

"PRIVACY NOT INCLUDED: FEDERAL LAW LAGS BEHIND NEW TECH," BY CHARLES ORNSTEIN, FROM *PROPUBLICA*, NOVEMBER 17, 2015

THE FEDERAL PRIVACY LAW KNOWN AS HIPAA DOESN'T COVER HOME PATERNITY TESTS, FITNESS TRACKERS OR HEALTH APPS. WHEN A FLORIDA WOMAN COMPLAINED AFTER SEEING THE PATERNITY TEST RESULTS OF THOUSANDS OF PEOPLE ONLINE, FEDERAL REGULATORS TOLD HER THEY DIDN'T HAVE JURISDICTION.

Jacqueline Stokes spotted the home paternity test at her local drugstore in Florida and knew she had to try it. She had no doubts for her own family, but as a cybersecurity consultant with an interest in genetics, she couldn't resist the latest advance.

At home, she carefully followed the instructions, swabbing inside the mouths of her husband and her daughter, placing the samples in the pouch provided and mailing them to a lab.

Days later, Stokes went online to get the results. Part of the lab's website address caught her attention, and her professional instincts kicked in. By tweaking the URL slightly, a sprawling directory appeared that gave her access to the test results of some 6,000 other people.

The site was taken down after Stokes complained on Twitter. But when she contacted the Department of Health and Human Services about the seemingly obvious

violation of patient privacy, she got a surprising response:
Officials couldn't do anything about the breach.

The Health Insurance Portability and Accountability Act, a landmark 1996 patient-privacy law, only
covers patient information kept by health providers,
insurers and data clearinghouses, as well as their
business partners. At-home paternity tests fall outside
the law's purview. For that matter, so do wearables like
Fitbit that measure steps and sleep, testing companies
like 23andMe, and online repositories where individuals can store their health records.

In several instances, the privacy of people using
these newer services has been compromised, causing
embarrassment or legal repercussions.

In 2011, for instance, an Australian company failed to
properly secure details of hundreds of paternity and drug
tests, making them accessible through a Google search.
The company said that it quickly fixed the problem.

That same year, some users of the Fitbit tracker
found that data they entered in their online profiles about
their sexual activity and its intensity — to help calculate calories burned — was accessible to anyone. Fitbit
quickly hid the information.

And last year, a publicly accessible genealogy database was used by police to look for possible suspects in
a 1996 Idaho murder. After finding a "very good match"
with the DNA of semen found at the crime scene, police
obtained a search warrant to get the person's name. After
investigating further, authorities got another warrant
ordering the man's son to provide a DNA sample, which
cleared him of involvement.

The incident spooked genealogy aficionados; AncestryDNA, which ran the online database, pulled it this spring.

"When you publicly make available your genetic information, you essentially are signing a waiver to your past and future medical records," said Erin Murphy, a professor at New York University School of Law.

The true extent of the problem is unclear because many companies don't know when the health information they store has been accessed inappropriately, experts say. A range of potentially sensitive data is at risk, including medical diagnoses, disease markers in a person's genes and children's paternity.

What is known is that the Office for Civil Rights, the HHS agency that enforces HIPAA, hasn't taken action on 60 percent of the complaints it has received because they were filed too late or withdrawn or because the agency lacked authority over the entity that's accused. The latter accounts for a growing proportion of complaints, an OCR spokeswoman said.

A 2009 law called on HHS to work with the Federal Trade Commission — which targets unfair business practices and identity theft — and to submit recommendations to Congress within a year on how to deal with entities handling health information that falls outside of HIPAA. Six years later, however, no recommendations have been issued.

The report is in "the final legs of being completed," said Lucia Savage, chief privacy officer of the HHS Office of the National Coodinator for Health Information Technology.

None of this was useful to the 30-year-old Stokes, a principal consultant at the cybersecurity firm Mandiant. Four months after she filed her complaint with OCR, it suggested she contact the FTC. At that point, she gave up.

"It just kind of seems like a Wild West right now," she said.

PROTECTION OF CONSUMER-APP DATA VARIES

Advances in technology offer patients ways to monitor their own health that were impossible until recently: Internet-connected scales to track their weight; electrodes attached to their iPhones to monitor heart rhythms; virtual file cabinets to store their medical records.

"Consumer-generated health information is proliferating," FTC Commissioner Julie Brill said at a forum last year. But many users don't realize that much of it is stored "outside of the HIPAA silo."

HIPAA seeks to facilitate the flow of electronic health information, while ensuring that privacy and security are protected along the way. It only applies to health providers that transmit information electronically; a 2009 law added business partners that handle health information on behalf of these entities. Violators can face fines and even prison time.

"If you were trying to draft a privacy law from scratch, this is not the way you would do it," said Adam Greene, a former OCR official who's now a private-sector lawyer in Washington.

In 2013, the Privacy Rights Clearinghouse studied 43 free and paid health and fitness apps. The group found that some did not provide a link to a privacy policy and that many with a policy did not accurately describe how the apps transmitted information. For instance, many apps connected to third-party websites without users' knowledge and sent data in unencrypted ways that potentially exposed personal information.

"Consumers should not assume any of their data is private in the mobile app environment—even health data that they consider sensitive," the group said.

Consider a woman who is wearing a fetal monitor under her clothes that sends alerts to her phone. The device "talks" to her smartphone via wireless Bluetooth technology, and its presence on a network could be detected by others, alerting them to the fact that she's pregnant or that she may have concerns about her baby's health.

"That is a fact that you may not want to share with others around you—co-workers or family members or strangers in a café," said David Kotz, a computer science professor at Dartmouth College who is principal investigator of a federally funded project that is developing secure technology for health and wellness.

"We've seen this in the tech market over and over again," he added. "What sells devices or applications are the features for the most part, and unless there's a really strong business reason or consumer push or federal regulation, security and privacy are generally a secondary thought."

'WALKING THROUGH AN OPEN DOOR'

In Florida, Stokes is one of those people enamored with emerging health technologies. Several years ago, she rushed to sign up for 23andMe to analyze her genetic profile. And when she was pregnant with her daughter, she purchased a test that said it could predict the sex of the fetus. (It was wrong.)

The paternity test kit that piqued her interest earlier this year advertised "accuracy guaranteed" for "1 alleged father and 1 child." She remembers the kit costing about $80 at a nearby Walgreens. Such tests sell for about $100 online.

"It was kind of a nerdy thing that I was interested in doing," Stokes said.

The test was processed in New Mexico by GTLDNA Genetic Testing Laboratories, then a division of General Genetics Corp. Stokes was directed to log into a website and enter a unique code for her results. When they appeared, she noticed an unusual Web address on her screen, and she wondered what would happen if she modified it to remove the ID assigned to her.

She tried that and saw a folder containing the results of thousands of other people. She was able to click through and read them. "You wouldn't call that hacking," she said. "You would call that walking through an open door."

Stokes downloaded those publicly accessible records so that she would have proof of the lax security. "There were no safeguards," she said. She complained to the HHS Office for Civil Rights in early February. It answered in June, writing that the office "does not have authority to investigate your complaint, and therefore, is closing this matter."

Bud Thompson, who until last month was the chief executive of General Genetics, initially said he had not heard about Stokes' discovery. A subsequent email provided an explanation.

"There was a coding error in the software that resulted in the person being able to view results of other customers. The person notified the lab, and the website was immediately taken down to solve this problem," he wrote. "Since this incident, we have sold this line of business and have effectively ceased all operations of the lab."

The DNA testing company 23andMe, which helps people learn about their genetic backgrounds and find relatives based on those profiles, had a highly publicized lab mix-up in which as many as 96 customers were given the wrong DNA test results, sometimes for people of a different gender. A spokeswoman for the California-based company said she was unaware of any privacy or security breaches since that 2010 incident.

Kate Black, its privacy officer and corporate counsel, said that 23andMe tries to provide more protection than HIPAA would require.

"No matter what, no law is ever going to be narrow enough or specific enough to appropriately protect each and every business model and consumer health company," she said.

California lawmakers have twice considered a measure to prohibit anyone from collecting, analyzing or sharing the genetic information of another person without written permission, with some exceptions.

Then-Sen. Alex Padilla, who sponsored the bill, cited a California company that marketed DNA testing, including on samples collected from people without their knowledge. In a recent interview, he said that he was amazed state law did not protect "what's arguably the most personal of our information and that's our genetic makeup, our genetic profile."

The legislation failed. And Padilla, now California's secretary of state, remains concerned: "I don't think this issue is going away any time soon."

TOO MANY COMPLAINTS TO PURSUE

While Stokes was troubled by her experience, she was particularly disheartened by the OCR's response. "It was shocking to me to get that message back from the government saying this isn't covered by the current legislation and, as a result, we don't care about it," she said.

The agency's deputy director for health information privacy says there is no lack of interest. While it refers certain cases to law enforcement, OCR can barely keep up with those complaints that fall within its jurisdiction.

"I wish we had the bandwidth to do so," Deven McGraw said. "We would love to be able to be a place where people can get personalized assistance on every complaint that comes in the door, but the resources just don't allow us to do that."

For its part, the FTC has taken action against a few companies for failing to secure patients' information, including a 2013 settlement with Cbr Systems Inc., a blood bank where parents store the umbilical cord blood of newborns in case it is ever needed to treat subsequent diseases in the children or relatives. That settlement requires Cbr to implement comprehensive security and submit to independent audits every other year for 20 years. It also bars the company from misrepresenting its privacy and security practices.

But FTC officials say the number of complaints pursued hardly reflects the scope of the problem. Most consumers are never told when a company sells or otherwise shares their health information without their permission, said Maneesha Mithal, associate director of the FTC's division of privacy and identity protection.

"It may be done behind the scenes, without consumers' knowledge," she noted. "Those are the cases where consumers may not even know to complain."

1. Should such lists of DNA profiles be kept private?

2. How do Bluetooth-enabled health monitoring devices pose privacy risks?

"'DATABUSE' AS THE FUTURE OF PRIVACY?," BY JOSEPH JEROME, FROM THE *FUTURE OF PRIVACY FORUM*, OCTOBER 16, 2014

Is "privacy" such a broad concept as to be meaningless from a legal and policy perspective? On Tuesday, October 14th, the Center for Democracy & Technology hosted a conversation with Benjamin Wittes and Wells Bennett, frequently of the national security blog, Lawfare, to discuss their recent scholarship on "databuse" and the scope of corporate responsibilities for personal data.

Coming from a world of FISA and ECPA, and the detailed statutory guidance that accompanies privacy in the national security space, Wittes noted that privacy law on the consumer side is vague and amorphous, and largely "amounts to don't be deceptive and don't be unfair." Part of the challenge, as number privacy scholars have noted, is that privacy encompasses a range of different social values and policy judgments. "We don't agree what value we're protecting," Wittes said, explaining that government privacy policies have values and distinctions such as national borders and citizen/non-citizen than mean something.

Important distinctions are much less easier to find in consumer privacy. Wittes' initial work on "databuse" in 2011 was considerably broader and more provocative, applying to all data controllers — first and third party, but his follow-up work with Bennett attempted to limit its scope to the duties owed to consumers exclusively by first parties. According to the pair, this core group of duties "lacks a name in the English language" but "describe a relationship best seen as a form of trusteeship."

Looking broadly at law and policy around data use, including FTC enforcement actions, the pair argue that there is broad consensus that corporate custodians face certain obligations when holding personal data, including (1) obligations to keep it secure, (2) obligations to be candid and straightforward with users about how their data is being exploited, (3) obligations not to materially misrepresent their uses of user data, and (4) obligations not to use them in fashions injurious to or materially adverse to the users' interests without their explicit consent. According to Wittes, this core set of requirements better describes reality than any sort of "grandiose conception of privacy."

"When you talk in the broad language of privacy, you promise consumers more than the legal and enforcement system can deliver," Wittes argued. "If we want useful privacy policy, we should focus on this core," he continued, noting that most of these requirements are not directly required by statute.

Bennett detailed how data uses fall into three general categories. The first, a "win/win" category," describes where the interests of business and consumers align, and he cited the many uses of geolocation information on mobile devices as a good example of this. The second category reflects cases where businesses directly benefit but consumers face a neutral value proposition, and Bennett suggested online behavioral advertising fit into this second category. Finally, a third category of uses are when businesses benefit at consumer's expense, and he argued that regulatory action would be appropriate to limit these behaviors.

Bennett further argued that this categorization fit well with FTC enforcement actions, if not the agency's privacy rhetoric. "FTC report often hint at subjective harms," Bennett explained, but most of the Commission's actions target objective harms to consumers by companies.

However, the broad language of "privacy" distorts what harms the pair believe regulators — and consumers, as well — are legitimately concerned about. Giving credit to CDT for initially coining the term "databuse," Wittes defines the term as follows:

> [T]he malicious, reckless, negligent, or unjustified handling, collection, or use of a person's data in a fashion adverse to that person's interests and in the absence of that person's knowing consent. . . . It asks not to be left alone, only that we not be forced to be the agents of our own injury when

we entrust our data to others. We are asking not
necessarily that our data remain private; we are
asking, rather, that they not be used as a sword
against us without good reason.

CDT's Justin Brookman, who moderated the conversation, asked whether (or when) price discrimination
could turn into databuse.

"Everyone likes [price discrimination] when you
call it discounts," Wittes snarked, explaining that he was
"allergic to the merger of privacy and antidiscrimination
laws." Where personal data was being abused or unlawful
discrimination was transpiring, Wittes supported regulatory involvement, but he was hesitant to see both problems as falling into the same category of concern.

The conversation quickly shifted to a discussion of
the obligations of third parties — or data brokers generally — and Wittes and Bennett acknowledged they dealt
with the obligations of first parties because its an easier
problem. "We punted on third parties," they conceded,
though Wittes' background in journalism forced him to
question how "data brokers" were functionally different
from the press. "I haven't thought enough about the First
Amendment law," he admitted, but he wasn't sure what
principle would allow advocates to divine "good" third
parties and "bad" third parties.

But if the pair's theory of "databuse" can't answer
every question about privacy policy, at least we might
admit the term should enter the privacy lexicon.

1. Should privacy regulations protect against businesses benefiting at the expense of the consumer? Why or why not?

2. What obligation do data brokers have in protecting consumer privacy?

CHAPTER 4

WHAT ADVOCACY GROUPS SAY

As privacy rights become more entwined with civil rights, advocacy groups have stepped up to raise awareness about the ways technology can access and use our personal information. Groups like the Electronic Frontier Foundation (EFF) and the Sunlight Foundation are nonprofits that seek to research and advise on the ways big data can be used and abused. Many advocacy groups believe the collection of data needs to be more transparent. They believe that social media sites have an obligation to make their privacy policies clearer. Most advocacy groups are working toward giving people more control over how their data is used and shared. Groups like EFF also bring awareness to times when people's privacy rights have been violated and are, thus, an invaluable resource. The following articles will explain the position of various digital privacy advocacy groups and their goals.

"WHY AND HOW DOES TECHNOLOGY MATTER?," BY JULIA KESERÜ, FROM THE SUNLIGHT FOUNDATION, APRIL 9, 2013

A few weeks ago, our colleagues at the World Bank Institute held a highly informal and very motivating discussion on opening up contracts in fragile states. As many other similar conversations, this event also turned into an animated debate on the role of technology and why talking about the Internet instead of discussing ways to influence decision-making.

Without repeating all the arguments already stated by others, we intend to add a couple, hopefully constructive points to the debate around the effectiveness of technology in solving different kinds of complex problems. Most of our thoughts reflect the questions raised at the WBI event and other ongoing discussions.

Real change requires a healthy transparency ecosystem where all the bits are equally important. As a basis, we do need complete and quality government data that is released in a timely and appropriate manner in order to be able to make further conclusions to our societies and political systems. We also need developers, coders and hackers who love playing around information bits and are thrilled to turn datasets into easily searchable websites and engaging applications. But we need good investigative journalists too who can find real stories behind the facts, researchers and think tanks who make relevant conclusions to our societies, great advocates who know how to interact with government officers and reform-minded philanthropists who dare to invest

in riskier projects. None of these exist without the other
and none of them will bring about meaningful change
alone. Furthermore, the ongoing debate on the relevance
of technology weighed against the importance of advocacy seems to create a catch 22 situation: whenever
people start questioning the importance of technology,
they indeed end up exclusively talking about it, instead
of trying to find specific ways to involve citizens or best
practices to advocate for policy reforms.

There is no such thing as relevant or irrelevant data.
There may be certain priorities within specific cultural,
historical and political contexts and we surely have a
handful of bad examples from the OGP where countries
try to get away with ridiculously vague commitments but
that does not mean we should (or could!) decide which
government datasets are more/less relevant than the
others. Rather, the relevance or priority of datasets will be
dependent on the context: who is asking the question, the
problems the government is having, what kind of initiative is being created, whether there is a political element
to the question at hand, etc. It is also important to note
that a healthy transparency ecosystem does not require
strict priorities but strong actors in all fields and issue
areas, and a culture of enhanced collaboration between
these actors. A green NGO will most probably work with
environmental information, academics may be in the best
position to discuss ways of liberating research data and
anti-corruption organizations tend to focus on party and
campaign finance or lobbyist disclosure information.

Change may come painfully slow. The current hype
around technology and the seemingly conflicting arguments
on either the potential or the impotence of transparency

reflect our desire to make a change – immediately. And though many of us in the US and abroad are reasonably tired of and outraged by the hypocritical slowness of our governments, we have to understand and accept the fact that even if technology improves in a rapid manner, transforming fundamentals of politics and public administration simply does not happen overnight. Sometimes we even need a whole generation shift among our leaders to experience real change. Expecting that every single hackathon will deliver a final solution to a crucial social problem or hoping that better disclosure norms for instance in contracting processes will immediately cease corruption will result in a frustration that either cuts our efforts short or creates a vicious circle of questioning legitimacy again and again. Neither helps the cause.

Citizens as a homogenous group may not be the target group of all open government projects. When talking about citizen engagement in technology and transparency-related projects, many actors in the field tend to forget about the intermediary role media and other civil society organizations play in translating facts into stories/conclusions/policy reforms and keep thinking of citizens as their sole target group. Involving citizens in political processes is by all means the ultimate goal. But again: such a goal can only be achieved in a healthy ecosystem of strong mediators who translate the information. Furthermore, when designing open government projects, we have to acknowledge that there are different levels of possible interaction and while participatory budgeting may engage a critical mass of taxpayers, procurement monitoring is just never going to attract ordinary citizens the way it attracts companies or procurement experts. It surely does not mean that any of these efforts are more important than the others but that we have to remain realistic when defining our target groups and strategies associated with our open government projects. And since technology indeed engages more people than traditional advocacy, instead of idealizing or degrading it, we should embrace its potential to engage people who otherwise would never be interested in politics, decision-making and more abstract dimensions of democracy.

1. Why should data collection be used to help solve social problems?

2. Why should experts in technology and politics work together on issues such as these?

"WHY METADATA MATTERS," FROM SURVEILLANCE SELF-DEFENSE, BY THE ELECTRONIC FRONTIER FOUNDATION, AUGUST 8, 2010

In the context of digital communications, metadata is the digital equivalent of an envelope—it's information about the communications you send and receive. The subject line of your emails, the length of your conversations, and your location when communicating (as well as with whom) are all types of metadata. Metadata is often described as everything except the content of your communications.

Historically, metadata has had less privacy protection under the law in some countries—including the U.S.—than the contents of communications. The police in many countries can obtain the records of who you called last month more easily, for instance, than they can arrange a wiretap of your phone line to hear what you're actually saying.

Those who collect or demand access to metadata, such as governments or telecommunications companies, argue that the disclosure (and collection) of metadata is no big deal. Unfortunately, these claims are just not true. Even a tiny sample of metadata can provide an intimate lens into a person's life. Let's take a look at how revealing metadata can actually be to the governments and companies that collect it:

They know you rang a phone sex line at 2:24 am and spoke for 18 minutes. But they don't know what you talked about.

- They know you called the suicide prevention hotline from the Golden Gate Bridge. But the topic of the call remains a secret.
- They know you got an email from an HIV testing service, then called your doctor, then visited an HIV support group website in the same hour. But they don't know what was in the email or what you talked about on the phone.
- They know you received an email from a digital rights activist group with the subject line "52 hours left to stop SOPA" and then called your elected representative immediately after. But the content of those communications remains safe from government intrusion.

- They know you called a gynecologist, spoke for a half hour, and then searched online for the local abortion clinic's number later that day. But nobody knows what you spoke about.

Protecting metadata from external collection is a difficult problem technically, because third parties often need access to metadata to successfully connect your communications. Just like the outside of an envelope needs to be readable by a postal worker, digital communications often need to be marked with source and destination. Mobile phone companies need to know roughly where your telephone is in order to route calls to it.

Services like Tor and experimental projects like Ricochet hope to limit the amount of metadata that is produced by common ways of communicating online. Until laws are updated to better deal with metadata, and the tools that minimize it become more widespread, the best one can do is be aware of what metadata you transmit when you communicate, who can access that information, and how it might be used.

1. What is metadata?

2. Should metadata be kept private? Why or why not?

"EFF, ACLU SUE OVER WARRANTLESS PHONE, LAPTOP SEARCHES AT U.S. BORDER," BY THE ELECTRONIC FRONTIER FOUNDATION, SEPTEMBER 12, 2017

The Electronic Frontier Foundation (EFF) and the American Civil Liberties Union (ACLU) sued the Department of Homeland Security (DHS) today on behalf of 11 travelers whose smartphones and laptops were searched without warrants at the U.S. border.

The plaintiffs in the case are 10 U.S. citizens and one lawful permanent resident who hail from seven states and come from a variety of backgrounds. The lawsuit challenges the government's fast-growing practice of searching travelers' electronic devices without a warrant. It seeks to establish that the government must have a warrant based on probable cause to suspect a violation of immigration or customs laws before conducting such searches.

The plaintiffs include a military veteran, journalists, students, an artist, a NASA engineer, and a business owner. Several are Muslims or people of color. All were reentering the country from business or personal travel when border officers searched their devices. None were subsequently accused of any wrongdoing. Officers also confiscated and kept the devices of several plaintiffs for weeks or months—DHS has held one plaintiff's device since January. EFF, ACLU, and the ACLU of Massachusetts are representing the 11 travelers.

"People now store their whole lives, including extremely sensitive personal and business matters, on their phones, tablets, and laptops, and it's reasonable for them to carry these with them when they travel. It's high time that the courts require the government to stop treating the border as a place where they can end-run the Constitution," said EFF Staff Attorney Sophia Cope.

Plaintiff Diane Maye, a college professor and former U.S. Air Force officer, was detained for two hours at Miami International Airport when coming home from a vacation in Europe in June. "I felt humiliated and violated. I worried that border officers would read my email messages and texts, and look at my photos," she said. "This was my life, and a border officer held it in the palm of his hand. I joined this lawsuit because I strongly believe the government shouldn't have the unfettered power to invade your privacy."

Plaintiff Sidd Bikkannavar, an engineer for NASA's Jet Propulsion Laboratory in California, was detained at the Houston airport on the way home from vacation in Chile. A U.S. Customs and Border Protection (CPB) officer demanded that he reveal the password for his phone. The officer returned the phone a half-hour later, saying that it had been searched using "algorithms."

Another plaintiff was subjected to violence. Akram Shibly, an independent filmmaker who lives in upstate New York, was crossing the U.S.-Canada border after a social outing in the Toronto area in January when a

CBP officer ordered him to hand over his phone. CBP had just searched his phone three days earlier when he was returning from a work trip in Toronto, so Shibly declined. Officers then physically restrained him, with one choking him and another holding his legs, and took his phone from his pocket. They kept the phone, which was already unlocked, for over an hour before giving it back.

"I joined this lawsuit so other people don't have to have to go through what happened to me," Shibly said. "Border agents should not be able to coerce people into providing access to their phones, physically or otherwise."

number of electronic device searches at the border began increasing in 2016 and has grown even more under the Trump administration. CBP officers conducted nearly 15,000 electronic device searches in the first half of fiscal year 2017, putting CBP on track to conduct more than three times the number of searches than in fiscal year 2015 (8,503) and some 50 percent more than in fiscal year 2016 (19,033).

"The government cannot use the border as a dragnet to search through our private data," said ACLU attorney Esha Bhandari. "Our electronic devices contain massive amounts of information that can paint a detailed picture of our personal lives, including emails, texts, contact lists, photos, work documents, and medical or financial records. The Fourth Amendment requires that the government get a warrant before it can search the contents of smartphones and laptops at the border."

1. Should the government be allowed to search digital files at the border?

2. Why are the EFF and the ACLU suing the Department of Homeland Security?

"DHS'S MISGUIDED SOCIAL MEDIA RETENTION POLICY JEOPARDIZES FUNDAMENTAL FREEDOMS," BY MANA AZARMI, FROM THE CENTER FOR DEMOCRACY AND TECHNOLOGY, OCTOBER 20, 2017

Last month, the Department of Homeland Security (DHS) issued an alarming notice that DHS would now retain social media information in Alien-Files (A-Files). A-Files are government records, generated in the immigration context, that include the records of an individual as they pass through the United States immigration process, and are retained by DHS for 100 years after the individual's birthdate. Including a person's public social media postings in A-Files would expose them to routine scrutiny of their expressive activity and could have a major chilling effect on their participation in online life. After receiving immediate criticism for this announcement, DHS subsequently stated that "[t]he notice did not announce a new policy" and that it "simply reiterated existing DHS policy regarding the use of social media."

But retention of social media information should not be brushed off as 'business as usual' for DHS. This policy, and its negative consequences for the free expression and privacy rights of both immigrants and U.S. citizens, will affect many individuals: Alien Registration numbers, and their related A-Files, are assigned to immigrants, and also to certain categories of nonimmigrants who are granted employment authorization while they are visiting the U.S. Individuals with A-Files include naturalized citizens, lawful permanent residents (green card holders), immigrant visa holders, asylees, and special immigrant juveniles, and student visa holders with optional practical training.

CDT, along with 26 civil liberties, human rights and immigrants' rights organizations submitted a letter urging DHS not to retain social media information in A-Files.

The coalition opposes DHS's social media retention policy for multiple reasons:

RETENTION OF SOCIAL MEDIA INFORMATION WILL BE HIGHLY INVASIVE

A request for social media identifiers jeopardizes the right to anonymous speech online and benefits that stem from it, and exposes particularly sensitive information (like an individual's religious and political beliefs) to government scrutiny. The content retained under this notice is stored indefinitely, and may be broadly shared with government and private entities. Also, the number of people impacted by this policy is massive– all individuals with A-Files, and the individuals that interact with them on social media.

RETENTION OF SOCIAL MEDIA INFORMATION WILL CHILL FREE SPEECH AND FREE ASSOCIATION

Knowing that their social media content will or could be monitored, immigrants and the individuals that interact with them will feel pressure to self-censor, delete their social media accounts, and disengage from online spaces. Furthermore, citizens' engagement with immigrants may be inhibited due to their fear of surveillance, chilling the exercise of free association rights while stigmatizing and isolating immigrant communities.

RETENTION OF SOCIAL MEDIA INFORMATION INVITES ABUSE WITH LITTLE SECURITY BENEFIT

Online communications are incredibly contextual and prone to interpretive mistakes—and the stakes for immigrants are high: Mistakes could lead to findings of inadmissibility, removability (i.e. deportation), or a negative finding of good moral character (which can affect an individual's ability to naturalize, and attain other immigration benefits). Additionally, collection and retention of social media information creates the risk that improper negative inferences will be drawn from an immigrant's personal beliefs or opinions. In return, there is no reason to believe that this policy will yield a significant security benefit. Social media screening is easy for bad actors to circumvent; would-be wrongdoers can simply manipulate their social media presence to evade detection.

INDEFINITE RETENTION OF NATURALIZED CITIZENS' SOCIAL MEDIA INFORMATION EFFECTIVELY TREATS THEM AS SECOND-CLASS CITIZENS

Under this notice, the government will routinely and indefinitely retain stores of social media content associated with a naturalized citizen. DHS retains A-Files for 100 years after a person's birthdate, at which point they are archived, meaning that these records will effectively be retained by DHS for the rest of a naturalized citizen's life and beyond. The existence of a persistent dossier of a naturalized citizen's social media activity will mean that these citizens face scrutiny of their past social media record in ways that U.S.-born citizens will not routinely face.

THE NOTICE AND DHS'S STATEMENT LACK CLARITY

Many questions have been raised since the notice was issued. For example, it's unclear if the retention and screening of social media information will occur solely at the time an individual applies for a benefit, or if the surveillance be ongoing. This uncertainty creates confusion and fear for the immigrants impacted by this policy, which, as noted above, will manifest in a retreat from online communities at great personal and public cost.

CDT has worked with coalitions of human rights organizations to oppose DHS's past attempts to incorporate social media screening into visa processes, and recently opposed the State Department's regulations seeking to permanently incorporate social media screening into its "extreme vetting" procedures. These proceedings, and many others, are part of a troubling increase in government policies singling out immigrants for disfavored treatment and substantially expanding the government's routine collection, retention, and sharing of individuals' social media information. In the context of the past year, this DHS social media retention policy will unquestionably disproportionately impact Muslims and immigrant communities of color. CDT will continue to strongly oppose government collection, retention, use, and sharing of social media information.

1. Why does the coalition oppose DHS's social media retention policy?

2. How could government surveillance of social media pages negatively affect immigrants?

"EFF URGES SUPREME COURT TO TAKE ON UNCONSTITUTIONAL NSA SURVEILLANCE, REVERSE DANGEROUS RULING THAT ALLOWS MASSIVE GOVERNMENT SPYING PROGRAM," BY THE ELECTRONIC FRONTIER FOUNDATION, AUGUST 10, 2017

WASHINGTON, D.C.—The Electronic Frontier Foundation (EFF) asked the Supreme Court to review and overturn an unprecedented ruling allowing the government to intercept, collect, and store—without a warrant—millions of Americans' electronic communications, including emails, texts, phone calls, and online chats.

This warrantless surveillance is conducted by U.S. intelligence agencies under Section 702 of the Foreign Intelligence Surveillance Act. The law is exceedingly broad—Section 702 allows the government to conduct surveillance of any foreigner abroad—and the law fails to protect the constitutional rights of Americans whose texts or emails are "incidentally" collected when communicating with those people.

This warrantless surveillance of Americans is unconstitutional and should be struck down.

Yet the U.S. Court of Appeals for the Ninth Circuit, ruling in *U.S. v. Mohamud*, decided that the Fourth Amendment doesn't apply to Americans whose communications were intercepted incidentally and searched without a warrant. The case centered on Mohammed Mohamud, an American citizen who in 2012 was charged with plotting to bomb a Christmas tree lighting ceremony in Oregon. After he had already been convicted, Mohamud was told for the first time that information used in his prosecution was obtained using Section 702. Further disclosures clarified that the government used the surveillance program known as PRISM, which gives U.S. intelligence agencies access to communications in the possession of Internet service providers such as Google, Yahoo, or Facebook, to obtain the emails at issue in the case. Mohamud sought to suppress evidence gathered through the warrantless spying, arguing that Section 702 was unconstitutional.

In a dangerous and unprecedented ruling, the Ninth Circuit upheld the warrantless search and seizure of Mohamud's emails. EFF, the Center for Democracy & Technology, and New America's Open Technology Institute filed an amicus brief today asking the Supreme Court to review that decision.

"The ruling provides an end-run around the Fourth Amendment, converting sweeping warrantless surveillance directed at foreigners into a tool for spying on Americans," said EFF Senior Staff Attorney Mark Rumold. "Section 702 is unlike any surveillance law in our country's history, it is unconstitutional, and the Supreme Court should take this case to put a stop to this surveillance."

Section 702, which is set to expire in December unless Congress reauthorizes it, provides the government with broad authority to collect, retain, and search Americans' international communications, even if they don't contain any foreign intelligence or evidence of a crime.

"We urge the Supreme Court to review this case and Section 702, which subjects Americans to warrantless surveillance on an unknown scale," said EFF Staff Attorney Andrew Crocker. "We have long advocated for reining in NSA mass surveillance, and the 'incidental' collection of Americans' private communications under Section 702 should be held unconstitutional once and for all."

1. Why does the EFF think Section 702 of the Foreign Intelligence Surveillance Act is unconstitutional?

2. Should PRISM be used on non-American citizens?

"THE PERILS OF PERSONALLY IDENTIFIABLE PRE-CONVICTION DATA," BY DAMIAN ORTELLADO, FROM THE SUNLIGHT FOUNDATION, FEBRUARY 1, 2016

INTRODUCTION

Sunlight began examining criminal justice data almost a year and a half ago, as calls for nationwide officer-involved shooting statistics highlighted the fragmented nature of this data across the country. Sunlight unleashed a team of researchers, developers and policy analysts to scour the nooks and crannies of criminal justice data. After 18 months of investigating, researching, cross-referencing and tagging, we've collected over 9,000 databases of publicly available criminal justice data from all 50 states, the District of Columbia and the federal government. We call it Hall of Justice, and you can find it here.

The inventory was created to showcase the problems with data and highlight the need for more uniform and accessible standards in its publication and collection. In the process of developing it, our research uncovered troves of personally identifiable datasets. These discoveries made us wonder why so little congruence appeared to exist in how microdata were made public. Furthermore, we questioned the reasons behind its release, and whether the ethics of privacy and the right to a second chance were ever considered beforehand.

Unfortunately, those questions don't have simple answers. Unsurprisingly, standards for criminal justice data vary widely from state to state. California releases criminal justice microdata to academics conducting policy research, but scrubs personally identifiable information in online publications of data — even as the state requires police to make public a fairly comprehensive set of details about adult arrestees. Texas, worn down from processing FOIA requests, takes an alternative route and publishes inmates' personally identifiable information online — but buries the link so deeply in its corrections site that few realize this database exists.

Yet many questions remained unanswered, particularly around personal information and privacy. Where do we draw the line between citizens' rights to freedom of information and individuals' rights to privacy? Should governments differentiate between pre-conviction data — for example, mugshots or arrest records — and post-conviction data, such as records of inmates and their respective convictions? When personally identifiable information has been released in the name of the public good, how and when should governments protect against its exploitation for private gain?

MUGSHOTS

Let's take a concrete example: mugshots. Virginia's Freedom of Information Act requires local governments to release mugshots of adult arrestees. In Danville, Va., the local government complies with that requirement by posting two PDFs each week. The first lists the name, age, gender, race, address, date of birth and arrest location of each arrestee in the past week, as well as the charges filed. The second provides similar information, with accompanying mug shots.

This is problematic because of an increasingly common exploitative business model — one in which mugshots posted online by cities or counties are rehosted on private sites that charge users for their removal. Fortunately, many states, including Virginia, have passed legislation barring the practice of rehosting mugshots and soliciting payment for them to be taken down. Similar efforts have resulted in more complicated disagreements between lawmakers and the media, who, at least in South Carolina, believe that mugshots are a valuable part of reporting in the public interest. That dispute has bubbled up to the federal level, too. In 2012, the Reporters Committee for Freedom of the Press pressured former Attorney General Eric Holder to release mugshots under the Freedom of Information Act.

Some in law enforcement agencies have taken action unilaterally. A South Carolina jail decided to stop posting mugshots online in response to sites using extortion to profit off of arrestee information, while a Salt Lake County sheriff lambasted the practice as dragging people "through the mud for rest of their lives." The photographs cause lasting damage, and some seemingly value them as a form of entertainment.

That statement raises the question of why mugshots are considered a part of the public domain in the first place. CityLab unearthed a 1999 court ruling against *The New Orleans Times-Picayune*, which sued the Department of Justice to get a mugshot of former 49ers owner Eddie DeBartolo, Jr., and lost. The court summed up its decision with an argument that sheds light on the lasting impact of these artifacts.

> *A mug shot preserves, in its unique and visually powerful way, the subject individual's brush with the law for posterity. It would be reasonable for a criminal defendant, even one who has already been convicted and sentenced, to object to the public disclosure of his or her mug shot.*

Furthermore, the court noted that mugshots "contain information that is intended for the use of a particular group or class of persons." Principally, they serve as references for law enforcement to identify potential criminals in the case of repeat offenses, but even official uses of photographic data can have drawbacks when taken to an extreme.

The FBI's Next Generation Identification face recognition database will rely primarily on booking photos to match potential criminals with computer generated candidate profile lists that try to make educated matches with existing data. The Electronic Frontier Foundation warns that the technology has a great potential for false positives given the massive size of the dataset, potentially triggering criminal investigations on certain individuals for no reason other than likeness. Misuses of data by law enforcement are not unheard of either: Dozens of reports of Florida officers conducting unauthorized searches on the state's driving and vehicle information database have surfaced over the last several years, for example.

ARREST DATA

Daily arrest records are commonly posted online by local governments in a wide variety of formats. The Hartford (Conn.) Police Department, for instance, posts them via a data export from its records management system, where they include information on the suspect such as address, release status, charge and bond details, and notes on appearance. Similar examples exist at the county level: The corrections department of Orange County, Fla., uploads a daily jail booking report in PDF that appears to be slightly more processed, removing more personal elements such as address and appearance. Finally, some — like the Lafayette Parish Sheriff's Office in Louisiana — publish these data in a rather unsophisticated paragraph-like style directly onto its site.

An alternative to PDFs and plain text comes in the form of more user-friendly interfaces that allow visitors to search for arrest records by name, ID number, date or offense. Some, like the Harris County (Texas) Sheriff's Office, only display results if information specific to the individual is entered, while others, like the Mecklenburg County (N.C.) Sheriff's site, require only a letter or a date to return data on alleged offenders. Finally, others are provided in bulk. Fairfax County, Va., provides both a delimiter-separated version of its weekly arrest database, while West Virginia publishes a statewide bulk display of arrests by county. Either way, in most cases arrest data are only archived for a certain period, and then become unavailable online. In Prince William County, Va., records stay on the site for 60 days before they are removed, a fairly common practice by sheriffs.

In a country with constitutional due process requirements establishing a presumption of innocence, problematic policy questions emerge from these pre-conviction datasets. In California, for example, half of arrests do not result in charges or convictions. Tomorrow, we will examine the post-conviction datasets we discovered and how different stakeholders weigh their merits.

1. How can arrest records be used to exploit people? How can they be used to protect people?

2. Should arrest records be part of the public domain? Why or why not?

EXCERPT FROM "PROTECTING YOURSELF ON SOCIAL NETWORKS," FROM SURVEILLANCE SELF-DEFENSE, BY THE ELECTRONIC FRONTIER FOUNDATION, FEBRUARY 10, 2015

Social networking sites are some of the most popular websites and tools we use on the Internet. Facebook, Google+, and Twitter have hundreds of millions of users each.

Social networks are often built on the idea of sharing posts, photographs, and personal information. Yet they have also become forums for organizing and speech—much of which relies on privacy and pseudonymity. Thus, the following questions are important to consider when using social networks: How can I interact with these sites while protecting myself? My basic privacy? My identity? My contacts and associations? What information do I want keep private and who do I want to keep it private from?

Depending on your circumstances, you may need to protect yourself against the social media site itself, against other users of the site, or both.

Here are some tips to keep in mind when you're setting up your account:

REGISTERING FOR A SOCIAL MEDIA SITE

- Do you want to use your real name? Some social media sites have so-called "real name policies," but these have become more lax over time. If you do not want to use your real name when registering for a social media site, do not.
- When you register, don't provide more information than is necessary. If you are concerned with hiding your identity, use a separate email address. Be aware that your IP address may be logged at registration.
- Choose a strong password and, if possible, enable two-factor authentication. [...]
- Beware of password recovery questions whose answers can be mined from your social media details. For example: "What city were you born in?" or "What is the

name of your pet?" You may want to choose password recovery answers that are false. One good way to remember the answers to password recovery questions, should you choose to use false answers for added security, is to note your chosen answers in a password safe.

CHECK THE SOCIAL MEDIA SITE'S PRIVACY POLICY

Remember that information stored by third parties is subject to their own policies and may be used for commercial purposes or shared with other companies, for example, marketing firms. We know that reading privacy policies is a near-impossible task, but you may want to take a look at sections on how your data is used, when it is shared with other parties, and how the service responds to law enforcement requests.

Social networking sites, usually for-profit businesses, often collect sensitive information beyond what you explicitly input—where you are, what interests and advertisements you react to, what other sites you've visited (e.g. through "Like" buttons). It can be helpful to block third-party cookies and use tracker-blocking browser extensions to make sure extraneous information isn't being passively transmitted to third parties.

Some social networking sites, like Facebook and Twitter, have business relationships with data brokers in order to target advertisements more effectively. [...]

CHANGE YOUR PRIVACY SETTINGS ANCHOR LINK

Specifically, change the default settings. For example, do you want to share your posts with the public, or only with a specific group of people? Should people be able to find you using your email address or phone number? Do you want your location shared automatically? [...]

Remember, privacy settings are subject to change. Sometimes, these privacy settings get stronger and more granular; sometimes not. Be sure to pay attention to these changes closely to see if any information that was once private will be shared, or if any additional settings will allow you to take more control of your privacy.

YOUR SOCIAL GRAPH

Remember that you're not the only person who can give away potentially sensitive data about yourself. Your friends can tag you in photos, report your location, and make their connections to you public in a variety of ways. You may have the option of untagging yourself from these posts, but privacy does not work retroactively. You may want to talk to your friends about what you do and do not feel comfortable having them share about you in public.

1. How can social media compromise your answers to security questions?

2. What parts of privacy policies should you be sure to read before joining a social media site?

"DIGITAL SECURITY AND PRIVACY," FROM THE INFO-ACTIVISM TOOLKIT, BY WOMEN'S RIGHTS CAMPAIGNING

Digital security and privacy is crucially important.

For human rights advocates, journalists and activists as well as ordinary citizens, the possibility of your communications being monitored, or the threat of your personal identity or location being exposed, pose a considerable risk, especially if you are working with sensitive information or issues. A thorough digital security strategy is essential, as it will only be as strong as its weakest link. You don't want to simply lock the door to your house when all the windows are open!

Signs that digital security has been compromised can include:

- Passwords that change mysteriously
- Private messages that appear to have been read by someone else
- Websites that have become inaccessible from certain countries
- Officials revealing knowledge about private correspondence, including dates, names or topics discussed

- Signs that mobile phone conversations have been monitored

DO I NEED TO BE CONCERNED ABOUT THIS?

Yes. Such scenarios could compromise your projects or expose you or your contacts to censorship, surveillance or persecution. The technology required to compromise someone's digital security is quite simple.

BASIC PRECAUTIONS

Regularly updating your computer's operating system, installing reliable anti-malware software, and doing regular back-ups are the most important basic precautions to take.

FIVE KEY POINTS FOR DIGITAL SECURITY ON THE INTERNET

1. Be anonymous

Anonymity software such as Tor is useful when you do not want to reveal which websites you have visited. Tor bounces your connection between several random volunteer computers in order to prevent even your ISP (Internet Service Provider) or government-level observers from knowing what you are doing on the internet. However, do not use Tor when sending or receiving sensitive information to or from insecure websites. Unless you are connected to a website that supports HTTPS, it is possible for one of the volunteer computers to monitor the content as it loads.

You can also use Tor to hide your identity from the websites you visit or to bypass Internet filters. These tools are useful when you need to access websites that are blocked; for example for research, or in order to submit updates to web-based platforms such as Facebook.

2. Communicate through secure and/or encrypted channels

Just as the person delivering your mail – or any person with access to your mailbox - could potentially take a look at your personal letters, someone could monitor your internet communication while you log in to an insecure website.

2.1 Secure connections

To protect against this kind of attack, most popular web-based email, social networking, blogging, mapping, and video platforms offer secure connections, called HTTPS. You can check whether you have a secure connection to a webpage by looking for 'https://' (rather than just 'http://') at the beginning of your browser's address bar. Many web-based tools, however, do NOT use HTTPS to protect any information, other than your password, that you submit to or get from their websites.

As a result, if someone monitors your connection for long enough, they will learn what you have stored on that site. Your best defense against this is to use web-based tools that use HTTPS for all pages.

2.2 Encryption

You can complement a secure channel with an additional layer of protection – encryption. Encryption scrambles your message and makes it unreadable by anyone except the intended recipient. Protocols like PGP (Pretty Good Privacy) are now available as free and easy-to-install plugins for many major mail clients like Thunderbird and Outlook. PGP uses a combination of advanced cryptographic systems to not only scramble your message but also authenticate your identity to the recipient.

3. Have a strong password

Use our password checker to test the strength of your passwords.

- A password should be difficult for a computer program to guess.
- Make it long & complex: The longer a password is, and the wider the range of characters it uses (upper & lower case, numbers, punctuation), the less likely it is that a computer program would be able to guess it in a reasonable amount of time. You should try to create passwords that include ten or more characters. Some people use passwords that contain more than one word, with or without spaces between them, which are often called passphrases.

A password should be difficult for others to figure out.

- Make it practical: If you have to write your password down because you can't remember it, you may end up facing a whole new category of threats that could leave you vulnerable to anybody with a clear view of your desk or temporary access to your home, your wallet, or even the trash bin outside your office. Consider section using a secure password database such as KeePass. Do not share your password with anyone.
- Don't make it personal: Your password should not be related to you personally. Don't choose a word or phrase based on information such as your name, social security number, telephone number, child's name, pet's name, birth date, or anything else that a person could learn by doing a little research about you.

A password should be chosen so as to minimize damage if someone does learn it.

- Make it unique: Avoid using the same password for more than one account. Otherwise, anyone who learns that password will gain access to even more of your sensitive information.
- Keep it fresh: Change your password on a regular basis, preferably at least once every three months.

4. Keep regular backups

Each new method of storing or transferring digital information tends to introduce several new ways in which the information in question can be lost, taken or destroyed. Years of work can disappear in an instant as a result of theft, momentary carelessness, the confiscation of computer hardware, or simply because digital storage technology is inherently fragile. There is a common saying among computer support professionals: "it's not a question of if you will lose your data; it's a question of when." So, when this happens to you, it is extremely important that you already have an up-to-date backup and a well-tested means of restoring it.

Although it is one of the most basic elements of secure computing, formulating an effective backup policy is not as simple as it sounds. It can be a significant planning hurdle for a number of reasons: the need to store original data and backups in different physical locations; the importance of keeping backups confidential; and the challenge of coordinating among different people who share information with one another using their own portable storage devices.

5. Cover your traces

When using public online tools like Facebook, and Twitter for mobilization or coordination, remember that the information you store on such platforms becomes, to some extent, the property of the operators, and that many of these tools expose more information than you might think.

When you entrust a sensitive project to operators of any online tool, read their privacy policies or user agreements. Remember that even the most enlightened policy leaves your information under the direct control of the platform's administrators, who would be able to share, sell or misplace that information without your permission or knowledge. Even if you terminate your account, many of these sites do not actually delete the content you have posted or the personal information you have provided.

Unless it is important that you use a particular commercial service, either because of its accessibility or because doing so helps you blend in with lower-profile users, consider some of the rights-progressive alternatives: Blip.tv instead of YouTube; riseup.net rather than Gmail. If you have the technical resources, you can also run your own web-based services.

If you use commercial platforms, take precautions to protect yourself from malicious individuals who know how to dig up private information on such services. This is particularly true of social network site platforms such as Facebook and MySpace. Develop a thorough understanding of the privacy features that are built into these platforms, and think about the kinds of information that you might unintentionally reveal about yourself or your organization; for example, your real name, where you live, the places to which you travel and details about upcoming events or meetings. If monitored over a long time, such information can also provide a picture of your habits and working practices.

One helpful technique is to create multiple accounts on any web-based service that you use, allowing you to use different accounts or profiles for different projects, and to maintain test accounts that you can use to 'spy' on yourself. Your privacy is better protected if you are able to check, in different ways, what is revealed about your account; for example, through web searches or people who hold special access privileges. Me & My Shadow allows you to interactively visualize how many pieces of personal information you are revealing when you use the internet.

1. How can you make a strong password?

2. Why is it important to take steps to avoid being tracked online if you are a political activist?

CHAPTER 5

WHAT THE MEDIA SAY

The role of the media is to explain issues around tech and privacy to the public and also inform them of ways to protect themselves. Ideally, good journalists can offer an impartial look at how technology can threaten or bolster our privacy rights. In the case of whistleblowers like Edward Snowden it was important for the media to give us the historical context for such actions. Part of the media's job is to alert the public to the dangers of new technological threats like doxxing, which is the release of someone's personal information with the intent that others use it to harass them. The media plays an important role in keeping the public informed while also asking tough questions about the future of privacy rights. The following articles will show what the media believes are the largest issues surrounding privacy rights and how people can protect themselves online.

"HOW TO PROTECT YOUR DIGITAL PRIVACY IN THE ERA OF PUBLIC SHAMING," BY JULIA ANGWIN, FROM *PROPUBLICA*, JANUARY 26, 2017

Every January, I do a digital tune-up, cleaning up my privacy settings, updating my software and generally trying to upgrade my security. This year, the task feels particularly urgent as we face a world with unprecedented threats to our digital safety.

We are living in an era of widespread hacking and public shaming. Don't like your political rivals? Beg Russia to hack them, and their emails mysteriously show up on Wikileaks. Don't like your ex-spouse? Post a revenge porn video. Don't like your video game opponents? Find their address online and send a SWAT team to their door.

And, of course, the U.S. government has the capability to do even more. It can spy on much of the globe's Internet traffic and has in the past kept tabs on nearly every American's phone calls. Like it or not, we are all combatants in an information war, with our data under constant siege.

So how can ordinary people defend themselves? The truth is you can't defend everything. But you can mitigate threats by reducing how much data you leave exposed for an intruder to grab. Hackers call this minimizing your "attack surface."

The good news is that there are some easy steps you can take to reduce the threat. Here is what I am doing this year:

UPDATING SOFTWARE

Every year, I ditch old buggy software that I don't use and update all the software that I do use to its most current version. Exploiting software with known holes is one of the ways that criminals install ransomware — which holds your data hostage until you pay for it to be released.

MAKING PASSWORDS LONGER

This year, I'm working to lengthen my passwords to at least 10 characters for accounts that I don't care about and to 30 characters for accounts I do care about (email and banking). After all, in 2017, automated software can guess an eight-digit password in less than a day.

Most importantly, don't re-use passwords. You don't have to think of unique passwords yourself — password management software such as 1Password, LastPass will do it for you. EFF technologist Jacob Hoffman-Andrews makes a very good case for password management software being the best defense against a phishing attack. (Phishing is how the email of John Podesta, Hillary Clinton's campaign chairman, got hacked).

SECURING COMMUNICATIONS

The good news is that it's never been easier to send encrypted text messages and make encrypted phone calls on the phone apps Signal and WhatsApp. However, please note that WhatsApp has said it will share users' address books with its parent company, Facebook, unless they opted out of the latest privacy update.

Of course, people who receive your messages can still screenshot and share them without your permission. On Signal you can make it slightly harder for them by setting your messages to disappear after a certain amount of time. In WhatsApp, you can turn off cloud backups of your chats, but you can't be sure if others have done the same.

PROTECTING MOBILE WEB BROWSING

The websites that you browse are among the most revealing details about you. Until recently, it was hard to protect mobile web surfing, but this year there are a lot of good options for iPhones. You can use privacy protecting standalone web browsers such as Brave or Firefox Focus, or install an add-on such as Purify that will let you browse safely on Safari. In an excess of excitement, I'm currently using all three!

Of course, blocking online tracking also means blocking ads. I hate to deny worthy websites their advertising dollars, but I also think it's unfair for them to sell my data to hundreds of ad tracking companies. Brave is building a controversial system that pays publishers for users' visits, but it remains to be seen if it will work. In the meantime, I try to subscribe or donate to news outlets whose work I admire.

DROPPING DROPBOX

You wouldn't leave your most sensitive documents in an unlocked filing cabinet, so why do you keep them in cloud services such as Google Drive and DropBox? Those companies have the keys to unlock your files. One option is to password protect your files before uploading them. But I prefer a cloud service that encrypts for me. In my usual overkill approach, I'm using Sync.com to synchronize files and SpiderOak for backup.

DELETING SOME DATA

Consider whether you really need to store all your old emails and documents. I recently deleted a ton of emails dating back to 2008. I had been hanging onto them thinking that I might want them in the future. But I realized that if I hadn't looked at them until now, I probably wasn't going to. And they were just sitting there waiting to be hacked.

RECONSIDERING INSTALLING CAMERAS AND MICROPHONES AT HOME

As Internet-enabled devices — ranging from smart hair-brushes to voice-activated speakers — invade the home, criminals are finding new ways to penetrate their defenses.

Hackers have spied on women through the womens' webcams and used networks of online cameras and other devices to bring down the Internet in Liberia. Like many people including the Pope and Facebook CEO Mark Zuckerberg, I have covered the cameras on my computers with stickers and magnetic screens to avoid peeping Toms. But until device makers heed the Federal Trade Commission's security recommendations for inter-net-enabled devices, I won't introduce new cameras and microphones into my home.

OPTING OUT OF DATA BROKERS

Fears that President Donald Trump might build a Muslim registry prompted thousands of Silicon Valley tech workers to sign a pledge stating that they wouldn't participate in building any databases that profile people by race, religion or national origin. But only three of the hundreds of data brokers that sell lists of people have affirmed that they would not participate in a registry. Two other data brokers told a reporter that the price for such a list would range from about $14,000 to $17,000.

It's not easy to remove personal data from the hundreds of data brokers that are out there. Many of them require you to submit a picture of your photo ID, or write a letter. But if you do it — as I did two years ago — it is worth it. Most of the time when a new data broker emerges, I find that my data is already removed because I opted out from the broker's supplier. I compiled a list of data broker opt-outs that you can use as a starting point.

TAKING A DEEP BREATH

The size of the problem and the difficulty of the solutions can be overwhelming. Just remember that whatever you do — even if it's just upgrading one password or opting out of one data broker — will improve your situation. And if you are the subject of a hateful, vitriolic internet attack, read Anita Sarkeesian's guide to surviving online harassment.

1. Why is deleting old emails a good idea?

2. Why take steps to protect your information online when large-scale surveillance programs exist? Do you believe it makes a difference?

"EDWARD SNOWDEN DEMONSTRATES THE POWER OF BREAKING RANKS," BY KEN BUTIGAN, FROM *WAGING NON-VIOLENCE*, JUNE 13, 2013

When Edward Snowden surfaced just days after releasing documents last week detailing the National Security Agency's wholesale data-mining of Internet content and telephone traffic, the very thing he wanted to avoid happened: There was a sudden shift from a riveting focus on unparalleled threats to privacy — and the way the Bush and Obama administrations have largely gutted the Fourth Amendment's constitutional protections from unreasonable search and seizure — to Snowden himself.

The media and members of Congress largely turned its magnifying glass on the putative criminality of the whistleblower and thus gave themselves permission to step more gingerly around the glaring elephant in the room: that the United States has poured billions of dollars into building a vast capacity to spy on U.S. citizens — and people around the globe — secretly, comprehensively and virtually without accountability.

WHAT THE MEDIA SAY

Snowden, who seems clear about the personal consequences he will likely face for taking this action, felt driven by what he learned about this vast surveillance system to jump ship. By so doing, he not only brought more sunlight into yet another murky corner of the infrastructure of the ever-expanding U.S. global and domestic control — part of the dizzying flurry of recent revelations about drones, special operations and kill lists — he has taught us, just as Bradley Manning, Julian Assange and Daniel Ellsberg did, the critical importance of breaking ranks.

Successful nonviolent movements depend on people breaking ranks: questioning, demurring, disobeying, defecting and withdrawing support. In most cases, this entails a slow process in which a significant percentage of the population gives up its fidelity to the status quo and finds itself shifting. As the late social movement theorist Bill Moyer put it, the population may not agree with the movement's answer, but it is beginning to question — and even gradually abandon — the traditional one.

This can be more than switching positions. In some cases it can herald a transformation of identity. To no longer support a policy, an institution or a whole system can signal a profound metamorphosis. We no longer identify with this policy. We no longer draw meaning or comfort from going along. At times we break ranks not only with a particular social issue but also from the system, and its assumptions and values, that created and sustained it.

This is one reason nonviolent change is slow. A population does not change its mind easily. It is a gradual process of trying on this new identity — of getting comfortable enough with it to face the external and internal blowback that comes from going AWOL psychologically, politically or culturally.

Sometimes, though, the long-term process of a whole society doing this is given a jolt by a particular example: the individual conscientious objector, the abstainer, and the resister — the one who, as Gandhi said, pits "one's whole soul against the will of a tyrant." Not only do the Edward Snowdens of the world help the rest of us see more clearly the realities we are up against — in this case, the institutionalization of unfettered, massive data collection on and profiling of the population — they can shock us into realizing that part of our job description as human beings is our obligation to withdraw our passive or active consent from such policies.

Daniel Ellsberg — who released the Pentagon's secret study of the war in Vietnam in 1971 and faced 115 years in federal prison for doing so — wrote on Monday that "there has not been in American history a more important leak than Edward Snowden's release of NSA material." He said this for two reasons. First, because Snowden has revealed programs "that are blatantly unconstitutional in their breadth and potential abuse. Neither the president nor Congress as a whole may by themselves revoke the Fourth Amendment — and that's why what Snowden has revealed so far was secret from the American people."

Ellsberg quoted Sen. Frank Church, who headed the Senate hearings on U.S. intelligence agencies in the 1970s, when speaking of the NSA: "I know the capacity that is there to make tyranny total in America, and we must see to it that this agency and all agencies that possess this technology operate within the law and under proper supervision, so that we never cross over that abyss. That is the abyss from which there is no return." Ellsberg fears that Snowden's revelations establish that we, indeed, have entered the abyss. In fact, he goes so far as to say we've become "the United Stasi of America," echoing but also surpassing East Germany's massive system for spying on its citizens.

But there is another reason Ellsberg finds this a historic act: Snowden's action may spark an unexpected way out of the abyss. It may inspire others who have knowledge of what is really going on — including in Congress, the executive branch, and perhaps even in the intelligence agencies themselves — to create momentum "to bring NSA and the rest of the intelligence community under real supervision and restraint and restore the protections of the Bill of Rights."

In many settings over the past 40 years — and especially in the run up to various wars, like the 1991 Persian Gulf War and the U.S. war in Iraq — Ellsberg has urged government employees, contractors and policymakers with security clearances to break ranks with policies of impending destruction and go public. Retired Army Colonel Ann Wright — who was working in the State Department as the war in Iraq was brewing submitted her resignation one day before the invasion began — and a handful of others are examples of conscience trumping silence in this way.

But Ellsberg's hope does not only hinge on government officials. He believes in people power, something he has affirmed by engaging in innumerable acts of nonviolent resistance and stints in jail in the 40 years since releasing the Pentagon Papers. He invites all of us to break ranks. Without conscientious, coordinated, and creative nonviolent resistance, this superstructure of surveillance and control will simply become more sophisticated, intrusive and anti-democratic. The Roman satirist Juvenal asks in one of his plays, "Who will guard the guardians?" Ultimately, this is up to all of us.

1. What was important about Edward Snowden's leaked information?

2. How have views on surveillance changed since Snowden's leaks?

"OPEN GOVERNMENT AND CONFLICTS WITH PUBLIC TRUST AND PRIVACY: RECENT RESEARCH IDEAS," BY JOHN WIHBEY, FROM *JOURNALIST'S RESOURCE*, OCTOBER 22, 2013

Since the Progressive Era, ideas about the benefits of government openness — crystallized by Justice Brandeis's famous phrase about the disinfectant qualities of "sunlight" — have steadily grown more popular and prevalent. Post-Watergate reforms further embodied these ideas. Now, notions of "open government" and dramatically heightened levels of transparency have taken hold as zero-cost digital dissemination has become a reality. Many have advocated switching the "default" of government institutions so information and data are no longer available just "on demand" but rather are publicized as a matter of course in usable digital form.

As academic researchers point out, we don't yet have a great deal of long-term, valid data for many of the experiments in this area to weigh civic outcomes and the overall advance of democracy. Anecdotally, though, it seems that more problems — from potholes to corruption — are being surfaced, enabling greater accountability. This "new fuel" of data also creates opportunities for businesses and organizations; and so-called "Big Data" projects frequently rely on large government datasets, as do "news apps."

But are there other logical limits to open government in the digital age? If so, what are the rationales for these limits? And what are the latest academic insights in this area?

Most open-records laws, including the federal Freedom of Information Act, still provide exceptions that allow public institutions to guard information that might interfere with pending legal proceedings or jeopardize national security. In addition, the internal decision-making and deliberation processes of government agencies as well as documents related to personnel matters are frequently off limits. These exceptions remain largely untouched in the digital age (notwithstanding extralegal actions by WikiLeaks and Edward Snowden, or confidential sources who disclose things to the press). At a practical level, experts say that the functioning of FOIA laws is still uneven, and some states continue to threaten rollbacks.

LIMITS OF TRANSPARENCY?

A key moment in the rethinking of openness came in 2009, when Harvard University legal scholar Lawrence Lessig published an essay in *The New Republic* titled "Against

Transparency." In it, Lessig — a well-known advocate for greater access to information and knowledge of many kinds — warned that transparency in and of itself could lead to diminished trust in government and must be tied to policies that can also rebuild public confidence in democratic institutions.

In recent years, more political groups have begun leveraging open records laws as a kind of tool to go after opponents, a phenomenon that has even touched the public university community, which is typically subject to disclosure laws. A few news organizations have even come under scrutiny for publishing public records of debatable value. Further, public institutions do not always succeed in properly protecting privacy when they release, for example, sensitive court records. And beyond data releases, transparency also means allowing more government officials to speak with the media and public, a practice that has not been uniformly adopted at the state or federal level. In a 2012 paper published in the *UCLA Law Review,* "The New Ambiguity of 'Open Government,'" Harlan Yu and David G. Robinson offer a critique:

> *The vagueness of "open government" has undercut its power. Separating technological from political openness — separating the ideal of adaptable data from that of accountable politics — will make both ideals easier to achieve. Public servants can more readily embrace open data, and realize the full range of its benefits, when it is separated from the contentious politics of accountability. At the same time, political reformers — no longer shoehorned together with technologists — can concentrate their efforts on political accountability, whether or not they rely on new technology.*

Indeed, at a 2012 open data meeting among academics, activists and media members, many acknowledged the need to distinguish between improving public services through data — management or performance transparency — and addressing political corruption. The journalist Alex Howard, who covers the open government beat, has looked at the idea of "openwashing." As he has put it, "Simply opening up data is not a replacement for a Constitution that enforces a rule of law, free and fair elections, an effective judiciary, decent schools, basic regulatory bodies or civil society — particularly if the data does not relate to meaningful aspects of society."

A 2013 paper in *Politics & Society*, "Infotopia: Unleashing the Democratic Power of Transparency," by Archon Fung of the Harvard Kennedy School, presents the broad outlines of policy thinking around these issues, theorizing certain limits and advocating that there also be greater corresponding openness by corporations and other large non-public institutions. In general, the principles of "democratic transparency" mean that all large organizations that could threaten citizen interests should be induced to behave in socially beneficial ways. Information should be especially rich, deep and well organized on issues affecting citizens' interests, and it should be structured and designed to allow citizens — particularly sophisticated professionals and those with civic-minded organizations — to use it and take action.

Still, there is a tension that we are only just beginning to grapple with. Fung suggests that "open government" can become "naked government":

> *Some of the main users of open government data are journalists seeking to expose the waste or theft of public funds (one central form of accountability).*

*It is more difficult to use these data to register
the positive accomplishments of public action....
Naked government may thus systematically rein-
force negative perceptions of government. Simply
put, the politics of accountability often associated
with open government can amount to an Amazon
five-star rating system in which government can
only receive one or two stars.*

Fung notes that, in contrast to naked government,
the more useful idea of "targeted transparency" balances
these competing interests and works to address particular problems and advance shared values. For example,
"organizational 'report cards' that disclosure hospital
infection rates or patient outcomes for nursing homes ...
are justified primarily because they aim to improve particular outcomes." (For more, see "Targeting Transparency,"
in the journal *Science*, by Archon Fung, Mary Graham and
David Weil.)

PRIVACY AND OPENNESS

If there is a tension between transparency and public trust, there is also an uneasy balance between government accountability and privacy. A 2013 paper in the
American Review of Public Administration, "Public Pay
Disclosure in State Government: An Ethical Analysis,"
examines a standard question of disclosure faced in every
state: How much should even low-level public servants
be subject to personal scrutiny about their salaries? The
researchers, James S. Bowman and Kelly A. Stevens of
Florida State University, evaluate issues of transparency
based on three competing values: rules (justice or fair-

ness), results (what does the greatest good), and virtue (promoting integrity.) While generally favoring openness, their analysis also suggests:

- "Disclosure requirements applied across the board to all employees, with no distinction regarding the nature of the work or position involved, disregard important factors that deserve consideration."
- "Open salary policies could work best when (a) individual and group performance can be measured objectively, (b) performance measures can be developed for all job duties, and (c) effort and performance are related closely over short time periods."
- Publishing salaries can have consequences for workplace morale and harmony, interpersonal dynamics and workers' sense of privacy (and willingness to serve), leading to possible inefficiencies in the system. So these potential negative aspects of disclosure, particularly for lower-level employees, must be balanced against the public interest: "Releasing this information by position, not personal names, at least partially protects privacy and may also reduce conflict, especially for lower-level staff (the same can be said for salary ranges or 'pay bands'); indeed, 13 states provide salary data without identifying individual employees. Another alternative to full disclosure is to institute a threshold of ... $100,000."

The researchers suggest that more survey data is needed from institutions subject to disclosure rules and more case studies are required to investigate these evolving dynamics: "A variety of workplace issues such as conflict of interest for both the employee and the employer, divided loyalties for personnel seeking office, or the potential creation of a hostile work environment because of transparency laws will assist in understanding and addressing the pay-policy tensions."

1. How does transparency in government agencies promote accountability?

2. How can transparency affect public trust in institutions? Why is public trust important?

"MISPLACED CONFIDENCES: PRIVACY AND THE CONTROL PARADOX," BY MARGARET WEIGEL, FROM *JOURNALIST'S RESOURCE*, DECEMBER 5, 2012

The sense of security provided by safeguards such as sports helmets, seat belts and birth control pills often impels users to do things they wouldn't otherwise — ski faster, drive more recklessly or forgo condom use. Scientists call this tendency to respond to safety measures in ways that counteract protection "risk homeostasis," "the Peltzman effect" or "the control paradox." Does this effect also apply to user-controlled privacy safeguards on social networking sites?

Unease about Internet use is particularly acute among parents. A 2012 survey, "Parents, Teens, and Online Privacy," from Harvard's Berkman Center for

Internet and Society and the Pew Internet and American Life Project, finds that 81% of parents of younger Internet users express concern about the commercial exploitation of personal data; and 69% of parents of online teens are also concerned about the way a teen's reputation is being managed and the future implications of disclosures. The survey estimates that only 39% of parents of teens using social networking sites have helped their children adjust privacy settings.

A 2012 study published in *Social Psychological and Personality Science*, "Misplaced Confidences: Privacy and the Control Paradox," investigates the extent to which a user's sense of control influences the type and amount of personal information a user discloses online. The researchers, from Carnegie Mellon University, conducted three survey-based experiments with more than 450 participants from a North American university on the release or accessibility of personal information online. The goal was ultimately to see how, in practice, humans respond to increased privacy controls.

- "Paradoxically, participants were more likely to allow the publication of information about them and more likely to disclose more information of a sensitive nature, as long as they were *explicitly*, instead of *implicitly*, given control over its publication."
- In the first experiment, half of the participants were told that their answers would automatically be published in an online directory, while half were told that information from some participants would be randomly selected for inclusion. "People respond to manipulations of control over release of personal information in a paradoxical way: Even though lower control implied

lower objective risk of accessibility and usage of personal information by others, participants were less willing to disclose if they were provided less control over information release."

- During the second experiment, participants were told that the online directory would be accessible by just students, or by students and faculty. Participants expressed higher levels of concern when the publication of their online profile was uncertain than a directory accessible to both students and faculty.

- "Study two supports the central ideas that privacy concerns are affected by control over release of personal information and that reassurances about control … can distract people from concerns about potentially more hazardous accessibility."

- In the third experiment, participants could authorize the publication of each of their survey responses; half were given the option to share and publish explicit demographic information about themselves. Findings showed that virtually all participants granted publishing permission for their answers. "As long as people perceive control over the decision to publish personal information and the audience to whom access will be granted, they will indeed decide to publish it, even if the objective risks associated with disclosure increase dramatically."

The researchers stress that they are not asserting that individuals should be more concerned about online privacy — or that they should disclose less information online — only that the propensity to share more is influenced by structural factors such as site controls. "Control has become a code word employed both by legislators and government bodies in proposals for enhanced privacy production [but] higher levels of control may not always service the ultimate goal of enhancing privacy."

"Facebook's CEO Mark Zuckerberg has repeatedly stressed the role of privacy controls as instruments to have 'more confidence as you share things on Facebook,' while both Senator Kerry's bill proposal and the recent Federal Trade Commission's Privacy Report focus on giving users more [privacy] control," the researchers note. Given the findings of the study, such controls could have unintended effects. "The paradoxical policy implication of these findings is that the feeling of security conveyed by the provision of fine-grained privacy controls may lower concerns regarding the actual accessibility and usability of information, driving those provided with such protections to reveal more sensitive information to a larger audience."

1. How does a user's sense of control over privacy settings affect what they post on social media?

2. What unintended side effects could occur from giving users more privacy control?

"ANOTHER THREAT TO YOUR PRIVACY: THE WAY YOU WRITE," BY GLYN MOODY, FROM *PRIVACY NEWS ONLINE*, SEPTEMBER 13, 2017

The 'creator' of Bitcoin, Satoshi Nakamoto, has been identified. That, at least, is the claim in a recent article by Alexander Muse on Medium. But don't get too excited. The article not only fails to name him/her/them, Muse admits he doesn't know, either. All he will say is that the Department of Homeland Security (DHS) has discovered the true identity of Satoshi Nakamoto, but that it won't publicly confirm that fact. Not much of a story, you might think. But the real interest lies in how the DHS is alleged to have discovered Bitcoin's biggest secret:

> *"Throughout the years Satoshi wrote thousands of posts and emails and most of which are publicly available. According to my source, the NSA was able to the use the 'writer invariant' method of stylometry to compare Satoshi's 'known' writings with trillions of writing samples from people across the globe."*

The application of what is known as stylometry is only useful if you have other holdings of text linked to named individuals, which can be compared to a kind of stylistic fingerprint extracted from the texts under study. The problem is that Satoshi Nakamoto could be anyone, anywhere. That means stylometry is only likely to be helpful if you have a huge database of writings that includes everyone on the planet who is active on the Internet; people who are not online can probably be excluded since they are unlikely to have come up with something as inherently Net-based as Bitcoin. Although we are not generally aware of the fact, the NSA has just such a database, as the Medium article explains:

> "The NSA then took bulk emails and texts collected from their mass surveillance efforts. First through PRISM (a court-approved front-door access to Google and Yahoo user accounts) and then through MUSCULAR (where the NSA copies the data flows across fiber optic cables that carry information among the data centers of Google, Yahoo, Amazon, and Facebook) the NSA was able to place trillions of writings from more than a billion people in the same plane as Satoshi's writings to find his true identity. The effort took less than a month and resulted in positive match."

Again, leaving aside the fact that we are not told the supposed true identity of Bitcoin's creator, what is much more relevant for readers of this blog is that the NSA possesses trillions of texts written by billions of people, and can therefore fruitfully apply stylometry to work out the author of a document, provided it is substantial enough to make any match that is found statistically meaningful.

This means for practical purposes, that it is very difficult to write longer documents, or produce sets of smaller texts, anonymously. All the NSA needs to do is to calculate the stylometric fingerprint for a document or group of posts, and then compare it with the huge holdings of texts with identifiable authors in its database. Of course, the NSA will not expend large amounts of time and money doing so unless the document is of particular importance or – as in the case of Satoshi Nakamoto – the person sought is of particular note.

The quantity of digital data being generated continues to grow rapidly. As a result, the number of emails and social media posts that the NSA must store in order to have a comprehensive record of everyone's writing style is also growing rapidly. However, don't start hoping that the NSA will be overwhelmed, and forced to store only a portion of that data flood. Last December, Amazon announced a new service called the AWS Snowmobile:

> "This secure data truck stores up to 100 PB of data and can help you to move exabytes to AWS in a matter of weeks (you can get more than one if necessary). Designed to meet the needs of our customers in the financial services, media & entertainment, scientific, and other industries, Snowmobile attaches to your network and appears as a local, NFS-mounted volume."

The AWS Snowmobile is primarily designed to move petabytes – or even exabytes – from company data centers to Amazon's AWS cloud. But if Amazon can put that much storage in a single container, think how much the NSA might have crammed into its extensive facilities. Given that ten AWS Snowmobile containers can store an exabyte, the NSA could easily by running databases holding a zettabye or even a yottabyte. To put that in perspective, a Wired article on Amazon's product notes that a single AWS Snowmobile could hold five copies of the Internet Archive – effectively a backup copy of the Web, past and present – which contains "only" about 18.5 petabytes of unique data. Storing every email and social media post it intercepts is clearly quite feasible for the NSA.

Even if it doesn't (currently) do this, there is little doubt that the NSA, and other top intelligence agencies in other countries, have vast holdings of our digital activities. That's important not just for existing applications like stylometric analysis, but particularly for training future artificial intelligence systems. Indeed, most of the power of such AI tools comes from feeding in lots of relevant data to hone the system. Whatever algorithms the NSA and other spy agencies have developed, they are probably already pretty good at analyzing our digital lives thanks to the huge data stores available for training.

That's the bad news. Some good news is that just as stylometric analysis is gaining new power through the application of technology, so it can perhaps be defeated by technology. There's an open source project on GitHub called Anonymouth:

> "a Java-based application that aims to give users to tools and knowledge needed to begin anonymizing documents they have written.
>
> It does this by firing up JStylo libraries (an author detection application also developed by [the Privacy, Security and Automation Lab at Drexel University, Philadelphia]) to detect stylometric patterns and determine features (like word length, bigrams, trigrams, etc.) that the user should remove/add to help obscure their style and identity."

And so the great digital arms race continues, between those wanting to preserve their anonymity and privacy online, and those wishing to strip them away.

1. What is stylometry?

2. How do programs like Anonymouth prevent stylometric tracking?

"THIS IS HOW HACKERS CAN RUIN YOUR LIFE — AND HOW YOU CAN PROTECT YOURSELF," BY RHODESIA ALLEGRA, FROM THE *MOBILIZATION LAB*, SEPTEMBER 28, 2017

For years, cyber bullying was defined as being targeted by hateful commenters. Today, doxxing—hackers finding or stealing your private information and publishing it online, sometimes with threats of violence—is a clear and present risk to activists and campaigners. Doxxing protection and prevention may help protect you from digital mobs and even hostile government authorities.

In the summer of 2014, hackers tried to destroy the life of game designer Zoe Quinn. They stole and published online photos of her in the nude, as well as her home address, her cell phone numbers and her father's contact information. This unauthorized publication of personal information is called "doxxing," and it is becoming an increasingly common hazard of 21st century online life.

Quinn, a rising star in the gaming world, was the victim of an orchestrated harassment campaign carried out by a hateful mob. The widely-publicized incident, known as Gamergate, began when her ex-boyfriend, Eron

Gjoni, published a long online screed of over 9,000 words; in it he accused her, among other things, of having slept with a game reviewer in exchange for a positive review. According to Quinn, who details the experience of being doxxed in her new memoir, *Gjoni* "optimized" and marketed the copy to incite the hatred of its members. Many of the ensuing attacks against her were coordinated in online forums and in chat rooms.

This is what being doxxed meant for Zoe Quinn:

- Her social and email accounts were flooded with rape and death threats;
- Anonymous harassers made obscene and threatening phone calls to her and her father;
- Some of her online stalkers appeared at her home; she ended up having to move away, out of fear;
- Other online stalkers sent obscene and doctored images to her friends and supporters on social media;
- Someone edited her Wikipedia entry so that it showed her time of death;
- Former employers called her to ask if she had used them to obtain references for a new job. The calls turned out to be random people trying to squeeze more personal information about her from her former bosses.

As a consequence of these attacks, Quinn starting experiencing panic attacks, anxiety and violent nightmares. At one point, she was on the same dosage of medication that combat veterans take for PTSD. She is also in therapy.

HAZARDS OF DIGITAL LIFE

Once seen as an extreme case of online harassment, this kind of mob action and weaponization of personal information is emerging as a hazard of 21st century life online. People who engage in advocacy need to acknowledge this and learn how to protect themselves.

In May, 2017, Buzzfeed News reported that Trump supporters created a massive dossier on thousands of people who had signed an online petition against the president. The dossier contained the names, ages, addresses, phone numbers, religious and sexual orientations and social media accounts of the petition signers.

On 6 September, *The Intercept* published a detailed story on the infiltration of a group of neo-Nazis who were using chat rooms on a text and voice platform for gamers called Discord. The neo-Nazis had vacuumed up private information on more than 50 anti-fascist activists in 14 states from California to North Carolina; and they also discussed the need to doxx anyone who opposed their agenda — e.g., the leaders of the Southern Poverty Law Centre, leaders of any "activist groups," and journalists.

NOT ALL DOXXERS ARE NAZIS OR MISOGYNISTS

There are doxxers on the left of the political spectrum, too. Anti-fascists doxxed several of the neo-Nazis photographed marching at the August 2017 white supremacist rally in Charlottesville, Virginia. Some feminists and anti-fascist activists not only approve of doxxing but engage in it themselves.

And doxxing as a form of vigilante justice need not be political. Earlier this year, Anonymous published the home address of the family of provocateur Roosh V, the self-styled "pickup artist" whose views on women caused an uproar.

According to a national survey of 4,248 adults in the United States by the Pew Research Center released in July, 41 percent of Americans have been harassed online; in addition, 66 percent have seen others harassed. Pew characterizes harassment as offensive name-calling, purposeful embarrassment, physical threats, sustained harassment, stalking, and sexual harassment. Fourteen percent of those surveyed report that they've been harassed for their politics, and about one in 10 have been targeted as a result of their appearance, race, ethnicity or gender.

Samantha Silverberg, a therapist and co-founder of Online SOS, a new non-profit dedicated to supporting victims of online harassment and stalking, says that even if targets don't get doxxed, perpetrators often wield the threat of online harassment as a cudgel of psychological intimidation.

"One of the things that I see is threats to reveal personal information," she said in an interview. "I think it's a very common practice because it's an intimidation technique. If someone has their personal information revealed on the internet, that's a very scary thought for a variety of different reasons. The possibilities of the repercussions of that are so varied that I think it becomes a very easy threat for someone to make when they're feeling angry at someone else, or they want a resolution."

Three factors enable doxxers:

- the wealth of personal information about individuals that's legally trafficked online by data brokers (mostly in the United States);
- the digital trails we leave about ourselves through our uses of social media and other online services (see petition signing, above);
- our own poor security practices.

Zoe Quinn's story illustrates the point: She knew she should have used hard-to-guess passwords with, as she puts it "uppercase letters, numbers, symbols, the painted nails emoji, two numbers that haven't been invented yet and one terrible secret," but it was too bothersome, so she used "funkyfresh" for most of her accounts instead. This made it easy for hackers to gain access to her online accounts, which acted as stepping stones to discover even more information about her. For example, they accessed her long-forgotten eBay account, which included her shipping address.

DOXXING PROTECTION TOOLS AND NEXT STEPS

Quinn and her friend Alex Lifschitz have since established a non-profit organization to help victims of online harassment. Called Crash Override, the site offers a comprehensive range of guides and tools for improving one's online security and minimizing the risk of being hacked.

The "Crash Override's Automated Cybersecurity Helper," or C.O.A.C.H., is a guide that takes you through the steps toward improving one's online security.

Through a series of prompts, the guide leads you to take most of the basic actions that any security expert will tell you to take to secure your life online. These steps include:

- Installing a password manager (the tool offers links to LastPass, 1password, and KeePass. Some security professionals prefer 1password because it keeps all your vital information local, rather than in the cloud — where it is theoretically more vulnerable to hackers.)
- Using the password manager to generate unique, secure passwords for each of your online accounts on social media and services such as Paypal, eBay and Amazon.
- Implementing two-factor authentication to verify that you are indeed the owner of your online accounts.
- Checking your security settings on all of your social media services
- Reviewing what third party apps have access to your social media accounts, and limiting access to the ones you really use. The goal here is to reduce the risk getting hacked via a compromised app.
- Deleting old accounts on services that you don't use any more.

Crash Override includes a frightening list of things that hackers can do to exploit, intimidate and shame you online. They can, for example, break into your bank accounts or your Skype account – from which they can harass contacts associated with that account.

The bigger, more difficult task facing individuals online is deleting their presence from the data brokerage sites, of which there seem to be thousands. For those who can pay, Abine, a startup in Cambridge, Massachusetts offers DeleteMe; it is a service that erases one's presence from 14 different websites that store one's home address, age, and information about relatives. Abine requires clients to send them copies of their drivers' licenses in order to verify to the data brokers that they've been autho-rized to request the removal of an individual's information. But the service's reach is limited: they cannot remove all one's information from every single data broker.

Other useful tools on Crash Override's site: Statis-tics-backed talking points for victims of harassment that can be used to counter apathy from the police and others who might downplay their situation; thoughts on the pros and cons of contacting law-enforcement authorities; and an explanatory guide for employers of individuals who are being stalked and harassed (useful since many victims report that their employers don't understand what's going on and often end up thinking that the victims themselves are crazy.)

But even with all the precautions, it is not possible to reduce one's online vulnerability to zero. Adam Shostack, a security consultant, game designer and former principal program manager at Microsoft's Trustworthy Computing team, says. "You can do all of these things, and you should do them, but it's worth realizing that it's hard."

Shostack explains that the security professionals' mantra is: "Protect, Detect, Respond and Recover." Each organization has to think through these steps and weigh the costs and benefits of the lengths they will go to to protect yourself both online and off. That means carefully reviewing whether or not any given tool is appropriate for their particular situation.

For example, Signal, the widely-recommended encrypted voice and messaging app, might be a liability for an organization. "Signal is linked to your phone number. Your phone number is an incredibly useful bit of information," Shostack says, explaining that if a hacker or a member of a government security service obtains your Signal phone number, that person then has access to all your contacts.

Instead of Signal, activists might find Wickr a safer platform. It is a secure messaging app that does not use your phone number and defaults to all messages disappearing. The tradeoff is that Wickr is not as convenient to use as Signal. Shostack also suggests, if appropriate, delinking your social media name associated with your online activism from your legal identity documents, such as your driver's license.

Other useful resources for teams that want to review their security risks and procedures together include: Front Line Defenders and Tactical Technology Collective's "How To Assess Your Digital Security Risk" guide; and the Electronic Frontier Foundation's Surveillance Self Defense guide. The latter includes security guides, advice and procedures for numerous different kinds of communities and individuals and situations; Equality Labs has also published an anti-doxxing guide.

IS THERE SUCH A THING AS RIGHTEOUS DOXXING?

Doxxing a Nazi might seem like justice, but it is not very good tactics.

Preliminary research conducted by University of Michigan PhD candidate Lindsay Blackwell says that crowdsourcing collective responses to abusers online might be more effective than doxxing — and ultimately a choice that brings about positive results. "Bystanders who intervene now will play a critical role in shifting those norms for the better," she said.

In other words, a critical mass of people who publicly defend targets of harassment is a more constructive and effective means of pre-empting future, would-be doxxers. Participating in a positive action of this type, rather than doxxing for revenge, is also good tactics in that it minimizes the risk of exposing oneself to being doxxed in return.

Lindsey Blackwell elaborates:

"If 99 people are harassing Justine Sacco, and one person chimes in to condemn them, that could be risky for that one person," she explains. "But if 10 people are harassing her, and 90 other Twitter users say: 'Hey, that's not okay,' the odds are much better — and I'm hopeful we can start shifting norms in that direction. This won't work for people who genuinely wish to cause harm, of course, but ongoing research suggests that genuine 'bad actors' produce a minority of harassment online (same as offline misbehavior.)"

Zoe Quinn shares the view that doxxing for justice is a bad idea. The risks, she points out, are high: There are cases of doxxers having disseminated inaccurate information, or of targeting the wrong person. And once the mob has been unleashed, it's impossible to pull it back. "If mobs of people are known for one thing," she writes, "It's for being unable to dial it back once there's been an error."

In her book, Quinn's advice to would-be doxxers is to step back and question their motives, justifications and potential impact before becoming part of a mob.

In other words, doxxing as a means of effecting vigilante justice is problematic for both tactical and ethical reasons. It doesn't stop the bad guys; and it could very well hurt innocent people.

The evidence shows, and the experts agree, that the best means of protecting oneself from digital attacks is to implement best practices when it comes to security, and to align oneself with a strong online community composed of people who reject and are unafraid of standing up to attackers.

1. What is doxxing? Why is it dangerous?

2. Is doxxing always bad? Why or why not?

CHAPTER 6

WHAT REGULAR CITIZENS SAY

Privacy is something everyone should be concerned with. As social media has grown and changed so, too, has the kind of information people post. When Facebook first started, only students at certain schools could join. Back then, it was common for people to post photos of themselves doing silly things. When employers, teachers, and parents began joining Facebook it became socially unacceptable to post such photos. Technology changes the kind of information we feel is private and what we feel comfortable sharing. The internet also offers regular people a platform to post what they think about privacy rights. Things like blog posts from regular citizens can help shape public opinion about how social media should be used. The following articles show how everyday people are thinking about and working to change privacy rights.

"LIBERTY AND PRIVACY: CONNECTIONS," BY JOSEPH S. FULDA, FROM THE FOUNDATION FOR ECONOMIC EDUCATION, DECEMBER 1, 1996

If property is liberty's other half, privacy is its guardian. The right to privacy is essential to the preservation of freedom for the simplest of reasons. If no one knows what I do, when I do it, and with whom I do it, no one can possibly interfere with it. Intuitively, we understand this, as witness our drawing the curtains and pulling the window shades down when prowlers are about. The threat to freedom comes from both the criminal and the state, from any and all ways and means in which others forcibly overcome our will. Just as we do not want burglars casing our homes, we should fear the government's intimate knowledge of the many details of our daily lives.

Although equally critical to liberty, privacy rights, unlike property rights, are not enumerated in the Constitution (except for the fourth amendment's protection of persons, houses, papers, and effects from unreasonable searches), although throughout most of our history Americans have retained their right to privacy. Today, however, this right is insecure as the courts, except in a few cases, have been unwilling to find in privacy a right retained by the people as suggested by the ninth amendment's declaration and, despite *Lopez*,[1] have been unwilling to bar legislated invasions of privacy on the grounds that they are simply outside the scope of the few and well-defined powers granted by the Constitution to the Congress.

Nor is privacy from the snoop afforded that much more protection today. Few, indeed, are the invasions of privacy regarded as criminal, rather than tortious, and many are not actionable at all. Paradoxically, the argument has been that one has a liberty to invade the privacy of others, if there is no reasonable expectation for that privacy. That may sound reasonable, but it forms what engineers term a positive feedback loop: The more privacy is invaded, the less reason one has to expect privacy, and therefore the more it may be invaded. This faulty jurisprudential theory has single-handedly eviscerated tort law and rendered the only specific privacy protection in the Bill of Rights—that barring unreasonable searches—weaker and weaker. The proper response to this flawed reasoning is simple: People often expect, in the sense of justly demand, what they cannot expect, in the sense of predict. We may thus have a *right* to expect our privacy to be respected in the former sense, whether or not we may expect it to be respected in the latter sense. Expectations, in other words, must be defined against a *fixed* standard of reasonableness, not one programmed to continuously decay.

The most egregious governmental violation of our privacy lies with our tax system, which is frankly frightening, as the potential for the destruction of liberty arising from the reams of information returned annually to the government is vast. The government is told our family size, our occupation, our business associates— employers, employees, contractors, partners, and the like (and, if we report barter income, some of our friends, as well), our holdings (unless we realize neither profit nor loss from their transfer and, also, gain no income while we continue our ownership), our schooling (unless it is not relevant to our work), and our provisions for retirement. Although no one may expect such dire consequences, the potential exists for such diverse state initiatives as population control programs, mandatory occupational tracks, massive interference with freedom of association, and enforcement of any or all of these by threat of loss of our holdings. Without this tax-related information, such interferences would be impossible. It is no accident that totalitarian systems in which there is no freedom whatsoever also tolerate no privacy. For Big Brother to act, he must know, and state surveillance with spies everywhere was a staple of the now-fallen totalitarian regimes.

Nor are these concerns the idle musings of a libertarian alarmist. Buried deep in the pages of the *Federal Register* is news that the IRS is implementing a massive new initiative, styled Compliance 2000.[1] At the heart of the initiative is a huge database with personal information on every American gathered from records kept by other federal agencies, state and local authorities, private organizations and the media. The regulation giving notice of this massive new database, composed of records from cyberspace as well as more traditional sources, stated that Compliance 2000 is exempt from the notification, access, and content provisions of the Privacy Act [1974]. In other words, [t]his means that the IRS doesn't need permission to get information, doesn't need to show it to you, and doesn't need to correct the information even if it's wrong. Privacy groups such as EPIC (Electronic Privacy Information Center) and business groups such as the DMA (Direct Marketing Association) strenuously opposed the initiative, but it went forward anyway. The IRS hopes to look at what is consumed as a check on the self-reporting of what is produced, but the potential for abuse and, according to the DMA, for chilling legitimate businesses is obviously vast.

And, just as the state, in this initiative and more generally, threatens privacy, the market protects it. Consider the market institution of money. Money must be portable, durable, and limited in quantity but the value of money lies not only in what it can buy, but also in its protection of privacy. Under a barter regime, everyone I buy from knows what I produce, and everyone I sell to knows what I consume. In the cash economy, only my customers know what I produce and only those from whom I purchase know what I consume. That is why the black-market cash economies of the once-totalitarian regimes of Eastern Europe were synonymous with the bits and pieces of freedom that survived there. Of course, cash transactions protect privacy from the snoop as well as from the state. With my bank-issued MasterCard number, for example, any mail-order merchant can find out the sum of my purchases and cash advances, my last payment, my next due date and minimum amount due, and my credit line, for all it takes is the credit card number and my zip code, the former of which he must have to claim payment and the latter of which he must have to deliver the goods.

To a lesser extent, even the serial numbers on paper money abridge privacy, as those who engage in businesses the feds do not approve of, such as the drug trade, have found out. Bank holdings are even more vulnerable, because upon transfer of large amounts of cash from accounts (marked with an ever-present Taxpayer Identification Number), the government is immediately notified. The new industry now known as money-laundering provides nothing but privacy-protection services to the rather large market spawned by various federal prohibitions—and this simple fact holds, whatever one's opinion of the nature of the enterprises whose privacy is being protected.

Privacy is the great shield of freedom from interference. Everyone who savors freedom will champion the right to privacy.

1. How do privacy laws protect us from government intrusion? Is this important or not?

2. Should people expect privacy in the digital age?

"THE FBI WANTS TO BE EXEMPT FROM PRIVACY PROTECTIONS. WE NEED TO SAFEGUARD CIVIL RIGHTS," BY ROBYN CAPLAN, FROM *POINTS*, JUNE 21, 2016

The FBI recently announced its plan to request that their massive biometrics database, called the Next Generation Identification (NGI) system, be exempted from basic requirements under the Privacy Act. These exemptions would prevent individuals from finding out if they are included within the database, whether their profile is being shared with other government entities, and whether their profile is accurate or contains false information. Forty-four organizations, including Data & Society, sent a letter to the Department of Justice asking for a 30-day extension to review the proposal.

The NGI system contains biometric data for over 100 million individuals, including fingerprints and palm prints, iris scans, tattoos, and face-recognition-ready photos. The database contains biometric data for those who have been merely arrested, as well as those who have never been accused of a crime. Actions like applying for a job, a visa application, or even a driver's license can lead to your biometric data being made accessible to the FBI. Face-recognition photos are becoming particularly valuable due to their ubiquity. Though the NGI system contains only around 30 million photos (and face-recognition searches for law enforcement are currently restricted to the criminal identities portion of the database), the FBI has access to around 400 million such photos through agreements with individual states.

The NGI system has come under scrutiny for its potentially negative social impacts. Widespread and systemic discrimination has been found to impact whose data is included within the system. Minority groups are far more likely to get arrested than whites for the same crimes and tend to be over-represented within criminal biometric databases, increasing the likelihood that they or their family (through a process known as "familial matching") can be targeted and unduly affected by biometric tests and software known to have high rates of false positives.

But the exemptions that the FBI is proposing highlight another set of concerns stemming from this rapidly expanding database:

What are the effects on the First Amendment rights of those participating in public activities where law enforcement are using surveillance practices for purposes like public safety and crowd control?

The Privacy Act currently contains a provision (5USC 552A(e)(7)) that prohibits the government from tracking people's political activities. To be clear, the FBI is not asking for an exemption to this provision. However, the exemptions they are requesting—that individuals not be able to check whether they are in a database, with what agencies this information has been shared, and whether the information they hold is correct—would effectively prevent individuals from knowing when the 522A(e)(7) provision has been violated. The right to anonymous speech in both print and public spaces, is protected within the US by the First Amendment. These exemptions, in addition to vast improvements in facial recognition technologies, increase the likelihood that individuals could be identified at political events, eliminating the anonymity which can be fundamental to taking part in political protest and dissent without fear of retribution.

Advances in facial recognition technology heighten these concerns. Technology use by law enforcement within the US has actually lagged behind; governments internationally have become much more sophisticated about their use, particularly to increase security at major public events. Before the World Cup in Brazil in 2014, there were reports police would be using facial recognition goggles that could identify individuals at 400 feet and drones and helicopters outfitted with HD surveillance and infrared cameras. For the Olympic Games in Rio, Brazil is using much of the same technology and has also purchased four "monitoring balloons" with thirteen cameras that will send images to a centralized control center for analysis.

In the US, police departments are increasingly working to advance or adopt better facial recognition technologies, and states have been working with the NGI to enable access to face-recognition photos held by other agencies, such as Departments of Motor Vehicles. In 2013, the ACLU reported that at least twenty-six states have made driver's license photos available to police officers in what was referred to as a "face recognition fishing pond" to be used to identify crime suspects from images taken by security cameras. In California, the attorney general has publicly expressed interest in investing in and expanding use of new facial recognition software to identify individuals against mugshots.

With potential security threats posed in the wake of media coverage on attacks on civilians around the world, interest in facial recognition technology has only grown, tipping the balance between privacy concerns and security more towards the latter. There is another balance that must be struck though—between security and the right to anonymity to protect speech rights.

This balance between the need to protect anonymity in political discourse, and the desire to increase security particularly at public events, can be quite difficult to strike. The FBI does not clearly recognize this need. In their public presentations on their NGI technology, their experts used photos of 2008 Clinton and Obama campaign rallies to demonstrate how facial recognition technology could be used to identify individuals in crowds. Law enforcement is also having trouble walking this line. In 2014, there were reports that the Boston PD had taken part in a pilot program with IBM which used digital video surveillance and "situational awareness software" for two public events, Boston Calling in May 2013 and Boston Calling in September 2013.

The notion that the FBI and other law enforcement agencies would potentially use this technology against protestors and activists is not far-fetched. The FBI has flown surveillance flights over communities like Ferguson and Baltimore during recent periods of civil unrest—a practice FBI Director James Comey defended, saying it did not require a search warrant because the cameras are not focused on individuals. The FBI also has a long history of surveilling and policing social movements, particular civil rights activists, including Martin Luther King, Jr., and more recently, organizers of the Black Lives Matter movement. New technologies have increased these surveillance capabilities. An investigation by The Intercept found the Department of Homeland Security has been monitoring Black Lives Matter protestors since Ferguson, using location and social media data to produce minute-by-minute reports on protestors' movements during demonstrations.

It should also be noted that, depending on the state, biometric data will be kept within the system for many years. Los Angeles County, whose biometric system will be fully interoperable with the Next Generation Identification system maintains biometric information for arrestees within the system until they are 99 years old, if they have a criminal record, and until age 75, if they do not.

Since facial recognition technologies are rapidly advancing, the exemptions being proposed by the FBI could have wider effects in the future than they do now. Individuals would be unable to check whether they were in a database, or be given an opportunity to correct that information, even as technologies advance and become more powerful. At the moment, the FBI is only allowing public comment until July 6th. This is a very short amount of time to understand the very long-term consequences of these exemptions.

A special thank you to Ifeoma Ajunwa and Alvaro Bedoya who contributed ideas and edits to this post.

1. Does the fact that minorities are overrepresented in the NGI database make it an inherently biased system when it comes to law enforcement?

2. Does public surveillance limit one's right to public assembly? Why or why not?

"IT DOESN'T MATTER WHY DATA IS COLLECTED: IT ONLY MATTERS THAT IT IS," BY RICK FALKVINGE, FROM *PRIVACY NEWS ONLINE*, FEB 6, 2016

A lot of procedures for collecting personal information go to great length to explain why the data is being collected and how it will be used. Sadly, it's all for nothing. Any such safeguards are null and void, and the only thing that matters is that the data is collected.

We've all seen the privacy policies. We've seen the governmental fine print on how data will be used. It's just pretty print. It accounts for absolutely nothing. All that matters is that the data is collected.

A privacy policy may bind the corporation collecting the data about you, if you ask a lawyer. Maybe even if you ask a politician. What happens next is that the corporation goes bankrupt, all deals are off, and a liquidator looks at all the assets that can be monetized to pay off the bankruptcy debt as required by law. Those assets include the data collected about you.

A government may be equally honest when it collects data about you for the most benign of reasons. But come election day, that government is voted out of power, and the next administration discovers this cache of useful information about citizens that it re-purposes in ways that you would never have approved of at the time the data was collected.

In other words, it doesn't matter if you trust the good faith of the entity collecting data about you. It doesn't even matter if they have the purest of good faith from a strictly objective standpoint. Sooner or later, through legal, illegal, or violent means, those you trusted and who promised how the data will be used will no longer wield the required power over the data collected – and at that point, somebody else is calling the shots and rewriting the rules entirely to suit their interests.

The only concern when data is collected about you should be how that data can be abused in a worst case scenario, for that exact scenario is more likely than not to materialize.

There are many warnings of history here. One of the most horrifying, at the risk of pulling a Godwin, happened early last century as the Netherlands was collecting religion data as part of the population records. The reason was the most benign imaginable: to make sure that there were enough places of worship for everybody in the city, and at convenient distances from people's homes.

Surely nobody would object to such data being collected, to provide citizens with the best civic service possible?

Then, World War II came around. The new...
administration... found it very convenient to have religion
listed as part of the public population records, including
where all people lived. As a result, there were almost no
Jews at all in Amsterdam in 1945. Quoting Wikipedia:

> In 1939, there were some 140,000 Dutch Jews living
> in the Netherlands. [...] In 1945, only about 35,000
> of them were still alive. [...] Some 75% of the
> Dutch-Jewish population perished, an unusually
> high percentage compared with other occupied
> countries in western Europe. [...] The civil admin-
> istration was advanced and offered Nazi Germany
> a full insight in not only the numbers of Jews, but
> also exactly where they lived.

As horrible as this is, it's far too easy to dismiss it
because World War II was such an exceptional event
that could never possibly happen again. This is a mistake.
Most genocides are based off of public records, to the
extent that some of my fellow activists are doing research
into the field of *genocide-resistant identity cards.*

But even short of genocide, far short of genocide,
examples abound of how collected data has been horrifi-
cally repurposed. Let's take an example from modern-day
Sweden, which has one of the most extensive medical
databases for research into hereditary factors of PKU,
phenylketonuria, an inability to metabolize phenylala-
nine and therefore most artificial sweeteners. To assist
this research, a small blood sample has been taken from
every baby born after 1975. For strictly medical research
purposes into hereditary deficiencies.

That is, the blood sample database *was* strictly for
medical research, until a prosecutor's office realized they
could legally subpoena that database for DNA samples.

All of a sudden, without any public debate whatsoever, and merely at the initiative of a prosecutor's office, Sweden had created a DNA registry for law enforcement purposes of its entire population younger than 40 years of age. This registry remains today, and is the largest population DNA registry available to law enforcement anywhere on the planet.

Then, of course, you have the ordinary everyday but catastrophic database leaks, the ones that happen for all reasons from incompetence to malice. The recent leak from the Ashley-Madison dating service springs to mind.

The only thing that matters is whether data is collected at all.

1. What are the problems posed by the mispurpose of data?

2. Should the potential for data to be misused prevent it from being collected for useful purposes?

"REMOVING MY CHILDREN FROM THE INTERNET," BY RYAN MCLAUGHLIN, FROM *RYAN-MCLAUGHLIN.COM*, OCTOBER 14, 2013

About a week ago I began deleting all photos and videos of my children from the Internet. This is proving to be no easy task. Like many parents, I've excitedly shared virtually every step, misstep and milestone that myself and my children have muddled our way through.

To be honest, aside from making sure my Facebook privacy permissions were set, I hadn't given a whole lot of thought about sharing photos of the kids online. I've run this blog (in various formats) for about a decade, and sharing stuff on it was just what I did. What I've always done. It's sort of the point of it. And when in the last few years I've started blogging less and posting on Facebook more, I carried that same sense of "my life is an open book" with me to the social network.

My view on sharing photos of the kids has always been that the advantages of having an easy, centralized way of sharing photos with an extended family that are thousands of kilometers away outweighed the largely fictional threat of creepy people having access to them.

Several months ago I read Jeremy Goldkorn's rant on the subject. The article itself is excellent food for thought, but it was something in a post-script that resonated most with me:

> This is not only about privacy, it's also about your child's identity. We are human beings, not amoebas. How would you like it if your mother and father were in charge of your social media presence? That's what you're doing to your children.

At the time I was resistant to surrendering my position, which it appears many other readers of the article shared, that we now live in an extremely interconnected world where privacy is simply not the same as it used to be. I was looking at this strictly as a "privacy" issue, and I felt that keeping baby photos off the Internet was akin to bailing a tide pool.

In the months since, I've returned to topic a few times and found myself increasingly conflicted about things. In response to Jeremy, a mutual friend, John Biesnecker, added the following point to the discussion:

My wife and I do have ground rules for posting things, the most basic of which being never to post something that we'd be embarrassed about if our parents had posted something similar of us as a child. Is this making choices for our children? Yes, but so is virtually everything else one does as the parent of a small child—and some of those choices have real, material, immediate impacts on your child's life, impacts far greater, I would argue, than photos posted on Facebook.

You make a good point, though you don't expound on it, regarding the inevitability of one's identity showing up online. If this is indeed inevitable—and I agree that it is—then you're far better off controlling and shaping that narrative to the extent possible, rather than allowing it to be shaped for you by others.

Now it should be noted that John works for Facebook, and so one would assume that at least to some degree his views would align with the company's share-friendly ethos. However, he makes a good point about acting as a guardian of your child's online identity. And that brings us to my tipping point, Amy Webb's article on Slate, in which she shares the story of "Kate" and her share-happy parents:

> With every status update, YouTube video, and birthday blog post, Kate's parents are preventing her from any hope of future anonymity.

> That poses some obvious challenges for Kate's future self. It's hard enough to get through puberty. Why make hundreds of embarrassing, searchable

photos freely available to her prospective home-coming dates? If Kate's mother writes about a negative parenting experience, could that affect her ability to get into a good college? We know that admissions counselors review Facebook profiles and a host of other websites and networks in order to make their decisions.

There's a more insidious problem, though, which will haunt Kate well into the adulthood. Myriad applications, websites, and wearable technologies are relying on face recognition today, and ubiquitous bio-identification is only just getting started. In 2011, a group of hackers built an app that let you scan faces and immediately display their names and basic biographical details, right there on your mobile phone. Already developers have made a working facial recognition API for Google Glass. While Google has forbidden official facial recognition apps, it can't prevent unofficial apps from launching. There's huge value in gaining real-time access to view detailed information the people with whom we interact.

The easiest way to opt-out is to not create that digital content in the first place, especially for kids. Kate's parents haven't just uploaded one or two photos of her: They've created a trove of data that will enable algorithms to learn about her over time. Any hopes Kate may have had for true anonymity ended with that ballet class YouTube channel.

It forced me to really dig deep into why I share photos of my kids. Convenience? Sure. But there are convenient ways to share photos with family that don't run the risk of my kids unwittingly being used in advertisements or enshrined in Google Image searches for all time. While Zoë Stagg attributes it to ego, and while there is some science to back that up, I believe it was *pride* that was leading me to share.

Of course as pride goes, pride for your children is about the best kind there is. But after I put it in that context, I realized that the statement isn't "convenience > fleeting privacy" but rather "sharing pride < maintaining control". The pride I have for my children, and the resulting desire to share that with everyone that will listen (and "like" it) is not worth my children not having some modicum of control of their online identity and anonymity in the future. And so I've taken a tip from Amy Webb's article and expanded on something I had already done to a limited extent -- in addition to removing all media featuring them from the public Internet, I've created a *digital trust* of sorts. I've registered domain names and e-mail accounts for both boys. They may never use them, but at least they'll have the option to in the future, and it will give them a leg up on managing their digital identities when they reach an age when that will be important to them.

It may be inevitable that when they grow tall enough to have cameras and social media accounts they'll share every mundane and embarrassing detail of their lives, with Facebook and Google mining it all for advertisers. And so be it, such is the world in which we live. As their father I don't feel it's my job to insulate my children from the world, but rather it's to be the best custodian of their future selves I can be. Most of the time that means preparing them with the knowledge and tools they'll need, in this case it means understanding

I don't need to share my pride in them in digital media format for that pride to exist, and in the process it means protecting their digital identities long enough for them to make a mess of it themselves.

1. What responsibility do parents have toward protecting their child's social media image?

2. Should parents post photos and videos of their children on social media? Why or why not?

"HOW DOES PRIVACY DIFFER FROM ANONYMITY, AND WHY ARE BOTH IMPORTANT?," BY RICK FALKVINGE, FROM *PRIVACY NEWS ONLINE*, OCTOBER 2, 2013

Privacy and anonymity are two different concepts. They are both increasingly necessary as we get increasingly wiretapped and tracked, legally so or not, and it's import- ant to understand why they are an integral part of our civil liberties – why they are not just beneficial to the individual, but absolutely critical to a free society.

Privacy is the ability to keep some things to yourself, regardless of their impact to society. To take a trivial example, I lock the door when I go to the men's room – not because I'm doing something criminal or plotting to overthrow the government in the men's room, but simply because I want to keep the activity there to myself.

Research shows that it goes beyond a want and is a deep need – in all societies through history, people have created private spaces for themselves. Even in the most oppressive regimes, people have found a way to do something, something little, outside of prying eyes. This is rather telling.

When somebody says that only criminals have something to hide, they are plain wrong, as evidenced by this observation. Nobody would dream of making a keyboard for people with three arms, based on the simple fact that people don't have three arms. Yet, some surveillance hawks and cohorts are pushing for a society for people with no need for privacy – despite the fact that such people do not exist.

So privacy is a concept describing activities that you keep entirely to yourself, or to a limited group of people.

In contrast, anonymity is when you want people to see what you do, just not that it's you doing it. The typical example would be if you want to blow the whistle on abuse of power or other forms of crime in your organization without risking career and social standing in that group, which is why we typically have strong laws that protect sources of the free press. You could also post such data anonymously online through a VPN, the TOR anonymizing network, or both. This is the analog equivalent of the anonymous tip-off letter, which has been seen as a staple diet in our checks and balances.

It's obvious that these concepts – privacy and anonymity – are beneficial for the individual. But more importantly, it is in society's interest overall that every individual have these benefits. There is not just an individual benefit, but a collective benefit.

We've discussed a bit about the benefit of anonymity already – without anonymity in society, we've essentially lost the ability to keep our government in check. Simple as that. (Unless you want to pull a Snowden and flee halfway across the planet, but most people probably don't want to do that.)

The benefit and necessity of privacy are a bit more… hidden under the surface, and has to do with the fundamentals of democracy. In a democratic nation, we elect people to govern the country, including the full capacity to apply to force to individual citizens. Then, after a term of n years, we hold them accountable to their performance and re-evaluate whether they are fit to run the country or not.

If these leaders with the full capacity of a country's force had the ability to look into voters' homes, hearts, and minds, they would be able to hold voters accountable for their thinking and opinions, rather than the other way around. It becomes a complete 180-degree reversal of power. This is why privacy for the citizens and transparency for the government is paramount in a democratic society. And indeed, every society that has had it the other way around – transparent citizens and opaque government – have been, shall we say, low-satisfaction societies.

But anonymity isn't just important to blow the whistle on scandals. It can have profound catalyzing effects in developing society, in particular when breaking taboos or forwarding forbidden causes that were later vindicated.

For example, the events that led up to the formation of the United States centered early on something known as the Federalist Papers – documents and pamphlets nailed to trees throughout the then-British colony, documents advocating secession from England, independence, and a United States of America.

At the time, advocating such opinions publicly was high treason, not just punishable by death, but by a particularly gruesome type of death. It's not hard to see why the Federalist Papers were posted anonymously.

Thus, to illustrate the importance of anonymity not just to the individual but to society overall, the United States would not exist as a country if anonymity had not existed at the time preceding the Declaration of Independence.

Therefore, both privacy and anonymity – although different – are essential to a democratic society, not just to the individuals, but to society overall.

As an end note, it could be argued that nobody is really anonymous, but pseudonymous – that is, everybody has a name of some sort, even if it is one that cannot be connected to their common name. If you're uploading evidence of a government scandal under the nickname "Scarlet Whistleblower", are you really anonymous, or did you just create yourself a new name for this specific purpose? Arguably, the latter.

This can be seen as a philosophical issue with little real-world impact, and today, it is. However, the teen-agers growing up today are used to changing names online more frequently than underwear, and I predict the values around something as basic as a name can change dramatically over the next few generations.

1. How does anonymity encourage whistleblowers?

2. How are privacy and anonymity different? Explain how both are important to a functioning society.

"WHY STRONG ORGANIZATIONAL SECURITY CULTURE MATTERS (AND HOW TO CREATE ONE)," BY JASON TASHEA, FROM THE MOBILIZATION LAB, SEPTEMBER 13, 2015

You and your organization may not think much about digital security unless you have dealt with a security breach or threat. We've written recently about how you can use threat modeling and a wide range of online privacy tools to help protect yourself, your colleagues and data. However, tools, threat models and individual awareness are just ingredients in the security recipe. Almost every conversation we had with NGO staff and security experts came around to one common element: a strong organizational security culture.

Getting to a strong security culture is more amorphous than deploying a new tool. Digital security is about education and habit formation.

This article provides some concrete steps your organization can take to promote a strong security culture.

WE DON'T HAVE ANYTHING TO HIDE

When Glenn Greenwald, the reporter that introduced the world to Edward Snowden and his revelations, talks about privacy, inevitably there is a person in the room who says, "Why should I care? I've got nothing to hide." To this remark Greenwald calmly hands the person his email address and says, "What I want you to do when you get home is email me the passwords to all of your email accounts. Not just the nice, respectable work one in your name, but all of them. Because I want to be able to just troll through what it is you're doing online, read what I want to read and publish whatever I find interesting. After all, if you're not a bad person, if you're doing nothing wrong, you should have nothing to hide."

No one has taken Greenwald up on his offer.

Acknowledging that even the most upstanding of us have reason to care about our privacy is the first step to individual and organizational culture shift. However, converting yourself isn't enough. Whether you are the director of an NGO or a community organizer, security culture is about bringing others with you.

Bill Budington, a software engineer at the Electronic Frontier Foundation, put it clearly. "Privacy isn't an issue about you, it's about all of us."

Nick Sera-Leyva, Human Rights and Training Programs Manager at Internews, agrees. He starts with an ethical imperative, "It doesn't matter if you have nothing to hide, it matters if the people in your networks have anything to hide. You don't know. They may or may not. They are not obligated to be forthcoming about that, and you as an activist or journalist might not know what those things are."

While this imperative is a strong philosophical place to start from, Kristin Antin, Community Catalyst at the engine room, provides actionable steps forward. When working with organizational partners the engine room will first create common ground within the organization, then create a plan with the participants, and finally provide ongoing support where possible.

FIND COMMON GROUND

Shauna Dillavou, the executive director at CommunityRED, believes that security culture can't be created from a point of fear. "Scaring the pants off of someone just terrifies them. There's no clear call to action." Dillavou thinks that getting an organization on board requires meeting individuals and organizations on common ground.

Finding common ground requires a common language. As Allen Gunn, the executive director at Aspiration, notes, "Digital security means different things to different people. It means something different to an IT administrator as it does to an NGO director. The staff themselves might think it's opaque and intimidating."

Sera-Leyva works on creating that common language. As he travels through different communities, countries and professions he starts with the basics. Take the word "hacking" for example. "In a lot of countries the word 'hacking' means a bunch of green 1s and 0s and with a few key strokes the person can penetrate your entire digital world. Your email being hacked could be as easy as you using a simple password that someone can guess," explains Sera-Leyva.

Common language, however, isn't enough, says Antin. It's important to find how that organization's identity and values can intertwine with security.

Antin uses an organization she worked with as an example. This organization valued integrity and impact. Through discussions, the organization identified concrete ways that security connected to these values. The protection of their contacts' information was tied to their value of integrity, and protecting information about strategy and tactics was tied to their impact.

The engine room then worked with this organization to identify and roll out a plan to protect contact information and internal communications. Creating a plan also requires that common ground. "People need to know why there's a plan and why you are recommending a certain tool or approach," says Antin.

By understanding the organization, the engine room was able to leverage what the organization cared about and create an entry point to security culture.

FIND YOUR ALLIES, BUILD YOUR COMMUNITY & DON'T GIVE UP

If you follow the engine room's example and foster stakeholder buy-in and understanding during the planning stage you run a higher chance of success. During the planning process it's also important to identify your allies and early adopters.

These allies will help foster peer-sharing, which, as Gunn describes, is an important part of creating security culture. "As you're learning, you need to make sure your knowledge propagates amongst your organization."

All of this is to say, one training isn't enough. According to Sera-Leyva, trainers don't always have the resources to follow up after a training session. Finding champions within your organization is critical. Further, don't expect that everyone in your organization or social group is going to buy-in at first. By creating this core of support, it builds momentum that can help convert slower adopters and make your entire organization more secure.

Even by undertaking all of the efforts outlined in this series, creating a security culture is ever evolving. "You never arrive at security culture, you never get to secure. People need to understand what works today might not work tomorrow, and certainly wont work forever," opines Gunn.

But to Gunn this isn't grounds to become overwhelmed and just give up on security.

"If you give up, you're going to get what you expect: defeat. If you fight, you have a chance."

1. Why is having a shared language when discussing security matters important?

2. What is a security culture and how can you promote one?

CONCLUSION

Privacy is a human right. Everyone has something they hope to keep to themselves, but our technology encourages us to share more and more. As citizens we all have a role to play in shaping the future of privacy rights in America and elsewhere. Tech companies must be more vigilant when it comes to protecting data from being misused. It is also imperative that citizens push for transparency when it comes to government surveillance programs—as well as corporate ones.

A common thread in many of the articles included in this book is the need for citizens to control their own data. Protecting privacy doesn't mean an end to data collection. It means protecting the use of that data. The Health Insurance Portability and Accountability Act of 1996 (HIPPA) is a great example of how sensitive information can be collected and distributed safely. When citizens have control of their data it means they can make more informed choices and protect themselves from cyberattacks.

Strong privacy rights can also protect citizens from mass surveillance. As you have read, government surveillance does change people's behavior. It can prevent people from attending public events, which is a violation of their

First Amendment right to peaceably assemble. It can also prevent them from interacting with others online, which is a violation of their right to free speech. As a society we must decide if these forms of oppression are acceptable. It is up to citizens to demand that their representatives take a proactive stance on protecting individual privacy rights. Everyone should work together to build a society where privacy is valued and protected.

BIBLIOGRAPHY

Allegra, Rhodesia. "This Is How Hackers Can Ruin Your Life — And How You Can Protect Yourself." Mobilisation Lab, September 28, 2017. https://mobilisationlab.org/doxxing-protection-campaigners.

Angwin, Julia. "How to Protect Your Digital Privacy in the Era of Public Shaming." *ProPublica*, January 26, 2017. https://www.propublica.org/article/how-to-protect-your-digital-privacy-in-the-era-of-public-shaming.

Azarmi, Mana. "DHS's Misguided Social Media Retention Policy Jeopardizes Fundamental Freedoms." The Center for Democracy and Technology, October 20, 2017. https://cdt.org/blog/dhss-misguided-social-media-retention-policy-jeopardizes-fundamental-freedoms.

Boundless Political Science: Lumen Learning. "The Right to Privacy." Accessed January 16, 2018. https://courses.lumenlearning.com/boundless-politicalscience/chapter/the-right-to-privacy.

Brown, Deborah. "New UN Resolution on the Right to Privacy in the Digital Age: Crucial and Timely." *Internet Policy Review*, November 22, 2016. https://policyreview.info/articles/news/new-un-resolution-right-privacy-digital-age-crucial-and-timely/436.

Butigan, Ken. "Edward Snowden Demonstrates the Power of Breaking Ranks." *Waging Non-Violence*, June 13, 2013. https://wagingnonviolence.org/feature/the-power-of-breaking-ranks-edward-snowden-daniel-ellsberg-and-resisting-the-nsa.

Caplan, Robyn. "The FBI Wants to Be Exempt From Privacy Protections. We Need to Safeguard Civil Rights." *Points*, June 21, 2016. https://points.datasociety.net/the-fbi-wants-to-be-exempt-from-privacy-protections-we-need-to-safeguard-civil-rights-98f9a3cf419d.

Conley, John. "How Privacy Law Affects Medical and Scientific Research." *The Genomics Law Report*, September 1, 2015. https://www.genomicslawreport.com/index.php/2015/09/01/how-privacy-law-affects-medical-and-scientific-research.

Electronic Frontier Foundation. "EFF, ACLU Sue Over Warrantless Phone, Laptop Searches at U.S. Border." September 12, 2017. https://www.eff.org/press/releases/eff-aclu-media-conference-call-today-announce-lawsuit-over-warrantless-phone-and.

Electronic Frontier Foundation. "EFF Urges Supreme Court to Take On Unconstitutional NSA Surveillance, Reverse Dangerous Ruling That Allows Massive Government Spying Program." August 10, 2017. https://www.eff.org/press/releases/eff-urges-supreme-court-take-unconstitutional-nsa-surveillance-reverse-dangerous.

Electronic Frontier Foundation. "Protecting Yourself on Social
Networks." Surveillance Self-Defense. Updated February 10,
2015. https://ssd.eff.org/en/module/protecting-yourself-so-
cial-networks.

Falkvinge, Rick. "How Does Privacy Differ from Anonymity, and
Why Are Both Important?" *Privacy News Online,* October 2,
2013. https://www.privateinternetaccess.com
/blog/2013/10/how-does-privacy-differ-from-anonymi-
ty-and-why-are-both-important.

Falkvinge, Rick. "It Doesn't Matter Why Data is Collected: It
Only Matters That It Is." *Privacy News Online.* February 6, 2016.
https://www.privateinternetaccess.com/blog/2016/02/it-doesnt
-matter-why-data-is-collected-it-only-matters-that-it-is.

Falkvinge Foundation. "Why Metadata Matters." Updated August
10, 2015. https://ssd.eff.org/en/module
/why-metadata-matters.

Frazier, Connie, and David Nguyen. "#NotJustDorms. The Fourth
Amendment: Security, Privacy and Technology." *HigherEduca-
tionLaw,* June 17, 2017. http://www.highereducationlaw.org
/url/?currentPage=3.

Fulda, Joseph S. "Liberty and Privacy: Connections." Foundation
for Economic Education, December 1, 1996. https://fee.org
/articles/liberty-and-privacy-connections.

Gleibs, Ilka. "The Importance of Informed Consent in Social
Media Research." *London School of Economics and Political
Science Impact Blog*, March 27, 2015. http://blogs.lse.ac.uk
/impactofsocialsciences/2015/03/27/the-importance-of-in-
formed-consent-in-social-media-research.

Granick, Jennifer. "Data and Protecting the Right to Privacy."
The Center for Internet and Society, September 29, 2015.
http://cyberlaw.stanford.edu/blog/2015/09/data-and-protecting
-right-privacy.

Hinchliff Pearson, Sarah. "The Dynamic Balance Between Free
Speech and Privacy Interests." The Center for Internet and
Society, April 17, 2009. http://cyberlaw.stanford.edu
/blog/2009/04/dynamic-balance-between-free-speech-and
-privacy-interests.

Jerome, Joseph. ""Databuse" as the Future of Privacy?" Future of
Privacy Forum, October 16, 2014. https://fpf.org/2014/10/16
/databuse-as-the-future-of-privacy.

Keserü, Julia. "Why and How Does Technology Matter?"
The Sunlight Foundation, April 9, 2013. https://sunlightfoun-
dation.com/2013/04/09/why-and-how-does-technology-matter.

Laux, Christian. "Privacy Concepts: US v. EU." The Center for Internet and Society, September 21, 2007. http://cyberlaw.stanford.edu/blog/2007/09/privacy-concepts-us-v-eu.

Lee, Patrick G. "Can Customs and Border Officials Search Your Phone? These Are Your Rights." *ProPublica*, March 13, 2017. https://www.propublica.org/article/can-customs-border-protection-search-phone-legal-rights.

McLaughlin, Ryan. "Removing My Children From the Internet." *Ryan-McLaughlin.com*, October 14, 2013. http://blog.ryanm.ca/fatherhood/removing-children-internet.

Moody, Glyn. "UK Privacy Laws May Allow 230 Million Americans to Demand Personality Profiles Created by Trump's Big Data Ally." *Privacy News Online*, October 4, 2017. https://www.privateinternetaccess.com/blog/2017/10/uk-privacy-laws-may-allow-230-million-americans-demand-personality-profiles-created-trumps-big-data-ally.

Moody, Glyn. "Another Threat to Your Privacy: The Way You Write." *Privacy News Online*, September 13, 2017. https://www.privateinternetaccess.com/blog/2017/09/another-threat-privacy-way-write.

Morris, David. "Alaska Deftly Balances Privacy Rights and Public Interest." *On The Commons*, December 9, 2014. http://www.onthecommons.org/magazine/alaska-deftly-balances-privacy-rights-and-public-interest#sthash.tmBr4HKr.dpbs.

Obama, Barack. "Remarks by the President at the Federal Trade Commission." *The White House Archives*, January 12, 2015. https://obamawhitehouse.archives.gov/the-press-office/2015/01/12/remarks-president-federal-trade-commission.

Ornstein, Charles. "Privacy Not Included: Federal Law Lags Behind New Tech." *ProPublica*, November 17, 2015. https://www.propublica.org/article/privacy-not-included-federal-law-lags-behind-new-tech.

Ortellado, Damian. "The Perils of Personally Identifiable Pre-Conviction Data." The Sunlight Foundation, February 1, 2016. https://sunlightfoundation.com/2016/02/01/the-perils-of-personally-identifiable-pre-conviction-data.

Pfefferkorn, Riana. "On Social Media, How Can DHS Tell Who's an Immigrant?" The Center for Internet and Society, September 29, 2017. http://cyberlaw.stanford.edu/blog/2017/09/social-media-how-can-dhs-tell-who%E2%80%99s-immigrant.

Pilgrim, Timothy. "Privacy Matters." Office of the Australian Information Commissioner, 8 May 2014. https://www.oaic.gov.au/media-and-speeches/speeches/privacy-matters.

PoKempner, Dinah. "Privacy in the Age of Surveillance."
Foreign Policy In Focus, February 17, 2014. http://fpif.org/priva-
cy-age-surveillance.

Tashea, Jason. "Why Strong Organizational Security Culture Matters (And How to Create One)." *Mobilisation Lab*, September 3,
2015. https://mobilisationlab.org/why-a-strong-organisatio
nal-security-culture-matters-and-how-to-create-one.

Thomas, Jennifer. "Is Digital Connectivity Threatening Your Privacy?" *Pursuit*, March 14, 2017. https://pursuit.unimelb.edu.au
/articles/is-digital-connectivity-threatening-your-privacy.

Weigel, Margaret. "Misplaced Confidences: Privacy and the Control Paradox." *Journalist's Resource*, December 5, 2012. https://
journalistsresource.org/studies/society/internet/misplaced
-confidences-privacy-and-the-control-paradox.

Wihbey, John. "Open Government and Conflicts with Public
Trust and Privacy: Recent Research Ideas." *Journalist's Resource*,
October 22, 2013. https://journalistsresource.org/studies/poli-
tics/digital-democracy/government-transparency-conflicts
-public-trust-privacy-recent-research-ideas.

Women's Rights Campaign. "Digital Security and Privacy."
Info-Activism Toolkit. Accessed January 16, 2018. https://wom-
ensrights.informationactivism.org/en/basics/digital
-security-privacy.

CHAPTER NOTES

CHAPTER 2: WHAT THE GOVERNMENT AND POLITICIANS SAY

EXCERPT FROM "PRIVACY MATTERS" BY TIMOTHY PILGRIM

1. R Clarke, *What's 'Privacy'?* (2004) Australian National University www.anu.edu.au/people/Roger.

CHAPTER 6: WHAT REGULAR CITIZENS SAY

"LIBERTY AND PRIVACY: CONNECTIONS" BY JOSEPH S. FULDA

1. *United States v. Lopez*, 115 S. Ct. 1624 (1995). (Editor's note: see Eric Hagen, *Putting the Framers' Intent Back into the Commerce Clause*, pp. 813–816 of this issue.)

GLOSSARY

anonymity—When a person is not identified.

Brexit—The term for the possible departure of the United Kingdom from the European Union.

comity—An association of nations.

compliance—Fulfilling a demand.

cyber security—The protection of computer systems from theft or damages.

data—Information collected about people's online activities and daily lives.

doxxing—Publishing people's personal information online with the intent for others to threaten and harass them.

encryption—The process of sending an encoded message so that only certain people can see it.

jurisprudence—The theory or practice of law.

metadata—Information that provides information about other data.

public domain—Something that doesn't have a copyright and can be used by anyone.

ransomware—A program which steals users data and either denies access or threatens to publish it if the person doesn't pay their ransom.

SNS data—A social network service (SNS), which allows users to share information.

stylometry—The study of writing style.

tort—A wrongdoing that leads to a civil lawsuit.

FOR MORE INFORMATION

FURTHER READING

Carson, Brian. *Understanding Your Right to Freedom from Searches* (Personal Freedom & Civic Duty). New York, NY: Rosen, 2011.

Cunningham, Anne. *Privacy and Security in the Digital Age* (Current Controversies). New York, NY: Greenhaven Press, 2017.

Currie, Stephen. *How Is the Internet Eroding Privacy Rights?* (In Controversy). New York, NY: Referencepoint Press, 2014.

Currie, Stephen. *Online Privacy* (Issues in the Digital Age) New York, NY: Referencepoint Press, 2011.

Furgang, Kathy. *Understanding Your Right to Privacy* (Personal Freedom & Civic Duty). New York, NY: Rosen, 2011.

January, Brendan. *Information Insecurity: Privacy Under Siege*. New York, NY: Twenty-First Century Books, 2015.

Kemper, Bitsy. *The Right to Privacy: Interpreting the Constitution* (Understanding the United States Constitution). New York, NY: Rosen, 2015.

Kyi, Tanya Lloyd. *Eyes and Spies: How You're Tracked and Why You Should Know* (A Visual Exploration). Toronto, CA: Annick Press, 2017.

Merino, Noel. *Privacy* (Opposing Viewpoints) New York, NY: Greenhaven Press, 2015.

WEBSITES

Me and My Shadow
myshadow.org
This site helps you figure out how much data you share every day and offers ways to protect yourself.

Crash Override
crashoverridenetwork.com
This is a resource center and advocacy group for people facing online harassment.

INDEX